Statistics in Educational Research

Statistics in Educational Research

R.P. Pathak

KANISHKA PUBLISHERS, DISTRIBUTORS
NEW DELHI-110 002

KANISHKA PUBLISHERS, DISTRIBUTORS
4697/5-21A, Ansari Road, Daryaganj
New Delhi -110 002
Phones : 2327 0497, 2328 8285
Fax : 011-2328 8285
E-mail : kanishka_publishing@yahoo.co.in
kanishkabooks@gmail.com

Statistics in Educational Research

First Published-2007

Edition-2025

ISBN : 978-81-7391-968-8

PRINTED IN INDIA

Published by Madan Sachdeva for Kanishka Publishers, Distributors, 4697/5-21A, Ansari Road, Daryaganj, New Delhi-110002, Typeset by Sunshine Graphics, Delhi, and Printed at G.S. Printers, Delhi.

This book is dedicated
to
My Grand father (Dadaji)
at whose feel I learnt very much.

Preface

Statistics as a disciplined study is concerned with developing a coherent, logical probability, prediction and comprehensive outlook. Statistics, Education and Research have involved itself with a wide range of observations, measurement, tools, techniques and data.

This book has been designed and written primarily for use by the student who is offering compulsory paper Educational Research. Although attention has been focussed upon the student who is experiencing his initial format contact with statistics in research methodology, we have not been unmindful of the fact that others might profit from use of the book. It may well serve as a useful reference for students, teacher and teacher educators who are interested to use Statistics in Educational Research.

This book is of necessity, limited in scope and depth. We feel, however, that no important areas of statistics are omitted as far as the research student is concerned. The language used throughout the book is reasonably non-technical and concise. Numerous examples and illustrations have been drawn from the field of statistics in research in order to clarify important points and to enhance the reader's understanding of essential principles, concepts, methods and techniques of Educational Research.

The author wishes to place on record the contribution of his colleagues in different institutions namely NCERT, NUEPA, IGNOU and SCERT, who have been a real source of inspiration for this work.

I express heartfelt gratitude to my Vice-Chancellor Prof. Vachaspati Upadhyay for his inspiration and guidance.

My especial thanks are due to Prof. M.R. Chilana, Prof. S.D. Roka, Prof. P.N. Dave, Prof. G.L. Arora, Prof. B.R. Goel, Prof. S.S. Srivastava, Prof. A.K. Nagar, Prof. A.R. Rehman and Prof. K.K. Vashisth.

I acknowledge the cooperation expended to me by several friends and colleagues in the preparation of this book. I am especially indepted to my teacher for his kind help and guidance.

I must express my grateful appreciation to my wife Manorma without whose encouragement, devotion and sacrifice the publication of this book would not have been possible.

I also thanks several authors whose work have profusely drawn upon.

I also acknowledge to my students. They taught me more than they may realise.

I am grateful to Kanishka Publishers especially Mr. Vivek Chaturvedi for his cooperation in the publication of the book.

We hope the research scholars and teacher educators would find the book incredibly interesting and extremely useful. Any suggestions for the improvement of the book are always welcome.

R.P. Pathak

Contents

1

Concept of Statistics in Research

In everyday life we deal with data or observations in which statistics is used. For example: when we take our weights or measure of heights, when we scrutinise cricket Test scores of previous players, when we take note of the weather forecasts or when we compare the marks obtained in examinations by different students, we are mentally evaluating the various observations or measurements. Sometimes we use phrases like average student in a class, pass percentage in a given examination and the range of marks in a given subject. In all this, we are using statistical concepts. There is an element of statistics in all these processes of mental evaluation of observations or measurements.

MEANING AND DEFINITION OF STATISTICS

The word 'statistics' generally means 'accumulated numerical statements'. The science of statistics is an old science. It developed gradually and its field of application widened day-by-day. Hence, it is difficult to give an exact definition of statistics. Numerous definitions have been coined by different people. These definitions reflect the statistical angle and field of an activity.

The word 'Statistics' is known to have been used for the first time in "Elements of Universal Erudition". Here Statistics is defined as: "The Science that teaches us what is the political arrangement of all modern states of the known world."

Webster defined statistics as "the classified facts representing the condition of the people in a state, especially these facts which can be stated as numbers, or in table of numbers or in any tabular or classified arrangement."

H. Secrist defined statistics as "an aggregate of facts to a marked extent by the multiplicity of causes, numerically expressed, enumerated or estimated according to a reasonable standard of accuracy, calculated in a systematic manner for a pre-determined purpose and placed in relation to each other."

Croxtion and Cowden defined statistics as "the collection, presentation, analysis and interpretation of numerical data."

All these definitions indicate certain common characteristics of statistics. They show that statistics are aggregate of facts numerically expressed, that they are reasonable accurate, they are collected in a systematic manner and are influenced by a number of factors.

Need and Importance of Statistics in Research

Statistics are everywhere basic to research activities. To the extent that the researchers tend to keep alive their interests and research activities, they will necessarily lean upon their knowledge and skills in statistical methods. Let us briefly present the need and importance of statistics in research.

- Statistics permits the most exact kind of description that it is useful to any who can understand it when they read the symbols in terms of which these phenomena are described. Mathematics and Statistics are a part of our descriptive language.
- Statistics helps us to be definite and exact in our procedures.
- Statistics enables us to summarise our results in a meaningful and convenient form. Masses of observations taken by the researchers are meaningless and bewildering.
- Statistics provides an accurate device for bringing order out of chaos, for seeing the general picture in one's results.
- Statistics enables us to draw general conclusions and the process of extracting conclusions is carried out according to accepted rules. Furthermore, by means of statistical steps, we can say about how much faith should be placed in any

conclusion and about how far we may extend our generalization.

- Statistics enables us to predict how much of a thing will happen under conditions we know and have measured, e.g., we can predict the achievement of a student on the basis of his intelligence.
- Statistics enables us to analyse some of the casual factors underlying complex events. Thus, the role and place of statistics in research cannot be overemphasised.

The Frequency Distribution

A mass of data in its original form is called raw data. If we have obtained masses of items which are quantitatively expressed, we cannot readily see except how many items or observations we have that possess the quality we are interested in. Therefore, some system of organization of data is necessary.

THE ARRAY

A mass of data when put into an orderly arrangement by magnitude (ascending or descending) is called an array.

Example 1:

The following are the test scores of 50 students.

50	21	75	42	55	74	67	55	47	64
61	71	25	40	54	64	54	37	88	44
70	31	51	81	63	49	63	43	35	67
31	68	45	38	75	57	75	29	66	50
84	56	88	56	32	55	32	88	79	78

Solution:

The array is obtained by arranging the scores of all the 50 students in ascending order magnitude.

21	31	40	45	51	56	61	66	71	79
25	32	42	47	54	56	63	67	74	81
25	35	43	49	55	57	63	67	75	84
29	37	44	50	55	58	64	68	75	84
31	38	45	50	55	59	64	70	78	88

Discrete Frequency Distribution

While making the array, if we find that certain values occurs frequently, we can prepare discrete frequency distribution. Such a distribution is made by listing all the values occurring in the series and noting the number of time a value appear in the series.

Continuous Frequency Distribution

An important method of arranging and condensing data is that of the formation of continuous frequency distribution. Here, the various items of a series are classified into groups or classes and the number of items lying in each group or class is put against that group or class.

Number of Classes

We first decide about number of classes into which data are to be grouped. The number of classes should be between 5 and 20. However, the number of classes would also depend on the number of observations. With larger number of observations, we can have more classes.

Class Interval

The size of classes is known as class-interval. Class-intervals should, whenever possible, be of uniform size. After deciding about class-interval, say 5, we calculate the range (highest score minus lowest score) of scores to be grouped. From data given in example 1, range of scores is R = 88 – 21= 67. Let us apply the following formula to get the approximate number of classes.

$$\text{Number of classes} = \frac{R}{i} = \frac{\text{Range of Scores}}{\text{class interval}}$$

In the case of data given in Example 1, we can have $\frac{67}{10} = 6.7$ or 7 classes in whole numbers.

There are three methods of describing class limits. They are:

- Exclusive method.

- Inclusive method.
- True or actual class limits.

Exclusive Method

In this method, classes are so formed that the upper limit of one class is the lower limit of the next class. There is always continuity between two successive classes. For example, a score of 10 will be included in the class 10-20 and not in 0-10.

Inclusive Method

Unlike exclusive classes, inclusive classes include classes which are equal to upper limit of the class. In this method, classes are formed as 20-29, 30-39 and so on. The class 20-29 includes ten scores i.e., 20 to 29.

True of Actual Class Limits

We observe that in inclusive method, upper class limit is not equal to lower limit of the next class. Therefore, it is assumed that a score does not just represent a point on a continuous scale, but an interval of length of which the given score is the middle point. For example, a score of 10 upon a test represents the interval 9.5 to 10.5. Therefore, the true class limits for class 10-19 become 9.5 to 19.5.

Class Frequency

The number of items falling within the range of its interval is called frequency of that class. To facilitate counting these frequencies, we use 'Tally Bar'.

Tally Sheet

Tallying consists of setting up classes and representing by a sloping or vertical stroke, each item that falls in each class. When four such strokes have been made, a fifth diagonal or horizontal stroke intersecting all the four earlier strokes is drawn to represent the fifth item.

Let us prepare a frequency table by using exclusive method, inclusive method and true class limits for the data given in Example 1.

Exclusive Method	*Inclusive Method*	*True Class Limits*	*Tally Bar*	*Frequency*
20—30	20—29	19.5—29.5	IIII	4
30—40	30—39	29.5—39.5	~~IIII~~ I	6
40—50	40—49	39.5—49.5	~~IIII~~ III	8
50—60	50—59	49.5—59.5	~~IIII~~ ~~IIII~~ II	12
60—70	60—69	59.5—69.5	~~IIII~~ IIII	9
70—80	70—79	69.5—79.5	~~IIII~~ II	7
80—90	80—89	79.5—89.5	IIII	4
				N = 50

Example 1:

Suppose 35 students of the B.Ed. class obtained the following scores on an achievement test. Prepare a frequency distribution (using inclusive method) by taking the class interval as 30 and the lower limit as 39 of the lowest class.

43	55	43	71	41	62	65
58	47	62	69	47	51	55
73	70	51	65	71	42	55
39	72	45	60	59	40	49
65	59	59	55	67	67	72

MEASURES OF CENTRAL TENDENCY

Sometimes it is necessary to arrive at values which will be representative of the middle of the whole distribution of measures. For example, we may need to answer such questions as: How can we divide the class into two groups so that one group will contain the upper half of the class and the other group the lower half on the basis of certain reading – test scores? What is the average score on a reading ability test in a sixth grade class? What is the most common score in the class? These questions can be answered by using measures of central tendency. *Central tendency* is an average which represents all of the scores made by the group and as such gives concise description of the performance of the group as a whole.

Three most commonly used measures of central tendency are:

- Arithmetic mean.
- Median.
- Mode.

Arithmetic Mean

The arithmetic mean, commonly called the mean or average, is the most often measure of central tendency. It is defined as the sum of measures divided by the number of measures. Let us discuss the methods for finding out arithmetic mean in ungrouped and grouped data:

Computation of Arithmetic Mean

Arithmetic Mean in Ungrouped Data

If $x_1, x_2, x_3,$ .... x_n represent the values of the respective N items, then the arithmetic mean denoted by $\bar{X}$, of the given values, is defined as:

$$\bar{X} = \frac{x_1 + x_2 + x_3 + \ldots\ldots\ldots x_n}{N}$$

$$= \frac{\bar{X}}{N}$$

Where, $\frac{3}{5}\times 2$ = the arithmetic mean (read as 'x – bar')

ΣX = the sum of given observations

N = the total number of given observations.

Example 2:

Find the arithmetic mean for the following score:

91, 82, 65, 74, 68 and 87.

Solution:

$$\bar{X} = \frac{x_1 + x_2 + x_3 + \ldots\ldots\ldots x_n}{N}$$

$$= \frac{91+82+65+74+68+87}{6}$$

$$= \frac{467}{6}$$

$$= \mathbf{77.8}$$

Hence $\bar{X}$ **= 77.8**

Arithmetic Mean in Grouped Data (Discrete Variable)

We have already discussed about discrete frequency distribution. Now, the arithmetic mean for a discrete frequency distribution is obtained by using the following formula:

$$\bar{X} = \frac{\Sigma fx}{N}$$

here, Σfx = the sum of product of each score and its frequency.
N = the total number of individuals.

Let us apply this formula in following example.

Example 3:

Find the arithmetic mean for the following discrete frequency distribution:

(Scores) x	91	88	85	76	70	63
(Frequency) f	1	2	3	1	2	1

Solution:

Scores x	*Frequency* f	fx
91	1	91
88	2	176
85	3	255
76	1	76
70	2	140
63	1	63
	N=10	Σfx=801

$$\bar{X} = \frac{\Sigma fx}{N}$$

$$= \frac{801}{10}$$

$$= 80.1$$

Hence $\bar{X} = 80.1$

Arithmetic Mean in Grouped Data (Continuous Variable)

We have already discussed what we mean by continuous frequency distribution. There are two methods of computing arithmetic mean from continuous frequency distribution.

- Direct Method
- Short-cut Method

Direct Method

The formula for discrete frequency distribution can be used for grouped frequency distribution if x represents the mid-point of a class interval.

$$\bar{x} = \frac{\Sigma fx}{N}$$

where, x = the mid point of the class interval.
f = its respective frequency.
N = the total of all frequencies.

We can illustrate the use of this formula by taking data given in the following Example:

Example 4:

Calculate arithmetic mean for the following grouped frequency distribution:

Class interval:	23–25	21–23	19–21	17–19	15 –17	13 –15	11–13
Frequency:	3	4	5	6	5	4	3

Class interval	*Mid-points* x	f	fx
23—25	24	3	72
21—23	22	4	88
19—21	20	5	100
17—19	18	6	108
15—17	16	5	80
13—15	14	4	56
11—13	12	3	36
		N = 30	$\Sigma fx = 540$

For calculating the arithmetic mean, the following steps will be used:

- Find out the mid-point (x) of each class interval by taking the average of upper and lower scores of the class (Column 2 in the above solution).
- Multiply each mid-point (x) with its respective frequency to get the value of fx (Column 4 in above solution).
- Add all the values of fx to get Σfx.

Now apply the following formula to get $\overline{x}$.

$$\overline{x} = \frac{\Sigma fx}{N}$$

$$= \frac{540}{30}$$

$$= 18$$

Hence $\overline{x} = 18$

Short-cut Method

Arithmetic mean for the grouped data can be computed with the help of the following formula:

$$\overline{x} = a + \frac{\Sigma fd}{N} \times i$$

where,

a = assumed mean.

f = respective frequency of the mid-values of the class intervals.

i = class interval.

d = deviation of x from assumed mean a and divide by i, the class interval i.e.

$$d = \frac{x-a}{i}$$

N = total frequency.

The use of this formula can be easily understood through the data given in Example 4.

Solution:

Class Interval	*Mid-points x*	*f*	*d*	*fd*	
23—25	24	3	+3	9	+22
21—23	22	4	+2	8	
19—21	20	5	+1	5	
17—19	18	6	0	0	
15—17	16	5	–1	–5	– 22
13—15	14	4	–2	–8	
11—13	12	3	–3	–9	
		N = 30		$\Sigma fd = 0$	

The steps involved in the computation procedure may be listed as:

- Find out the mid-point of each class interval by taking average of the lower and upper scores of the class (Column 2 of the above solution).
- Near the centre of the distribution, choose an estimated mean class. We choose 17-19 class. However, the other classes could have been chosen. The mid-point of this class is 18 which will be the value of assumed mean '*a*'.
- '*d*' can be found for each class by subtracting '*a*' from *x* and then divide by *i* (As in column 4 in the above solution).
- The values of *fd* can be found by multiplying the *f* and *d* values (As in column 5 in the above solution).
- Find Σ*fd* by first adding the positive *fd* values (+22) and negative *fd* values (–22), thereby taking the numerical differences of these sub-totals (0).
- Now apply the following formula to get $\overline{X}$.

$$\overline{X} = a + \frac{\Sigma fd}{N} \times i$$

$$= 18 + \frac{0}{30} \times 2$$

$$= 18 + 0$$

$$= 18$$

Hence, $\overline{X} = 18$

Arithmetic Mean from Combined Groups

If there are K groups whose means $(\overline{X})$ and number of cases in each group (N_1) are known, we can compute their combined mean by using the following formula:

$$\overline{X}_{comb} = \frac{N_1\overline{X}_1 + N_2\overline{X}_2 + \ldots\ldots\ldots N_x\overline{X}_x}{N_1 + N_2 + \ldots\ldots\ldots N_x}$$

When only two groups are combined, then the combined arithmetic mean of the two groups can be obtained by using the following formula:

$$\overline{X}_{12} = \frac{N_1\overline{X}_1 + N_2\overline{X}_2}{N_1 + N_2}$$

Let us illustrate the use of this formula in Example 5.

Example 5:

25 boys and 15 girls in a class appeared in an examination. The average grade for boys and girls are 5 and 6 respectively. Find the average grade of all the 40 students in a class.

Solution:

Here, we are given that

$N_1 = 25 \qquad \overline{X}_1 = 5$

$N_2 = 15 \qquad \overline{X}_2 = 6$

Using the following formula, the combined average grade of all the 40 students will be:

$$X_{12} = \frac{N_1\overline{X}_1 + N_2\overline{X}_2}{N_1 + N_2}$$

$$= \frac{25 \times 5 + 15 \times 6}{25 + 15}$$

$$= \frac{125 + 90}{40}$$

$$= \frac{215}{40}$$

$$= 5.375 \ \overline{X}_{12}$$

Hence, X_{12} = 5.375 Grade.

Merits and Demerits of Arithmetic Mean

Merits and Demerits of Arithmetic mean following are:

- It is rigidity defined and easily understandable.
- Its computation is based on all the observations.
- It is also capable of being handled algebraically as its computation is based on all the observations made.
- Its value is least affected by fluctuations of sampling.
- The only demerit of an arithmetic mean is that it is highly affected by extreme values of a variable.

Median

The median is the midpoint in a distribution or the point which divides the distribution into two halves, with respect to frequencies. In other words, the median stands for that value of the variable which divides the total frequency into two equal parts, i.e. N/2 observations fall below and N/2 above the median.

Computation of Median

Median in Ungrouped Data

In order to find median in ungrouped data, we arrange the given ungrouped data in ascending or descending order of magnitude i.e. the data are first put in the form of an array which we have already discussed.

If number of scores (N) is odd, then median is exactly the $\frac{N+1}{2}$th value. If number of scores (N) is even, it is the mean of N/2th and $\frac{N+2}{2}$th values.

Let us illustrate it by taking an example.

Example 6:

Below are given the mental ages of 7 students:

7, 10, 6, 8, 9, 10, 11

Locate the median mental age.

Solution:

First of all, we arrange the given data in an ascending order of magnitude as given below:

6, 7, 8, 9, 10, 10, 11

Here what we see? We see that N = 7 which is an odd number. Now we will calculate median by using the following formula:

$$\text{Median} = \frac{N+1}{2}$$

$$= \frac{7+1}{2} = \frac{8}{2} = 4\text{th item in this arrangement, i. e., Median} = 9.$$

It is clear that 9 is also the midpoint in the above arrangement as exactly four observations are above and below this point.

When the number of items in a series is even, we can illustrate this by taking another Example 7.

Example 7:

Suppose we are given mental ages of 8 students:

7, 10, 6, 8, 13, 9, 10 and 11.

Find the median mental age.

Solution:

First of all, we arrange the given data in an ascending order as given below:

6, 7, 8, 9, 10, 10, 11, 13

Here, the number of observations (N) is 8 which is an even number. Which formula we will use for calculating median?

We will use $\frac{Nth}{2}$ value and $\frac{N+2th}{2}$ value. Thus there will be two middle values and their average will be the median. Therefore,

$$\text{Median} = \frac{4th \text{ value} + 5th \text{ value}}{2}$$

$$= \frac{9+10}{2}$$

Hence, median $= 9.5$

It is clear that the number of observations below and above the median would now be four.

Median in Grouped Data (Discrete Variable)

In case of a discrete frequency distribution, the median can be found by locating the median class so that exactly one half of the frequencies i.e. N/2 are below and one half above it. Thus median can be readily located with the help of a 'less than' cumulative frequencies as explained in the following Example:

Example 8:

Locate median score før a discrete frequency distribution:

Marks:	1,	2,	3,	4,	5,	6,	7,	8.
No. of students:	3,	5,	10,	12,	8,	6,	4,	2.

Solution:

Marks	*No. of students* f	*'Less than' Cumulative frequency C*
1	3	3
2	5	8
3	10	18
4	12	30
5	8	38
6	6	44
7	4	48
8	2	50
	N = 50	

Here, the total frequency is N = 50. Thus N/2 = 25. Now cumulating from the lower end, 25th frequency is obviously not among the first 3. 25th frequency comes in the fourth cumulation 30, upto variate 4. Hence 4 is the median score in this case.

Median in Grouped Data (Continuous Variable)

If the data is available in the form of continuous frequency distribution, we can find the median by first locating the class in which N/2th cumulative frequency lies. This class is known as median class.

Now the median value is located within this class using an interpolation formula written as follows:

$$\text{Median} = L + \frac{\frac{N}{2} - C}{f} \times i$$

where, L = the true lower limit of the median class.

$N/2$ = one half of the total frequency.

C = the cumulative frequency of the preceding median class.

f = the frequency of the median class.

i = class interval.

The use of this formula can be easily understood through the following Example:

Example 9:

Compute median for the following frequency distribution:

Scores:	20–29	30–39	40–49	50–59	60–69	70–79	80–89
No. of students:	4	6	8	12	9	7	4

Solution:

Scores Class Interval	*No. of students* f	*'Less than' Cumulative frequency* C
20—29	4	4
30—39	6	10
40—49	8	18
50—59	12	30
60—69	9	39
70—79	7	46
80—89	4	50
	N = 50	

The steps involved in the computation of median may be listed as:

- Find out less than cumulative frequency by adding the frequency of the class to cumulative frequency of the preceding class.
- Locate the median class in which N/2th frequency lies. In the example, N/2 = 25 and this frequency lies in 50 – 59 class. Hence, 50 – 59 is the median class.
- Now apply the following formula to get median:

$$\text{Median} = L + \frac{\frac{N}{2} - C}{f} \times i$$

$$= 49.5 + \frac{\frac{50}{2} - 18}{12} \times 10$$

$$= 49.5 + \frac{25 - 18}{12} \times 10$$

$$= 49.5 + \frac{7}{12} \times 10$$

$$= 49.5 + 5.83$$
$$= 55.33$$

Hence, median = 55.33

Merits and Demerits of Median

Merits and Demerits of Median following are:

- Median is also rigidly defined and easy to understand.
- Its computation is not based on all the observations. Hence, it is not capable of further algebraic treatment.
- It is not at all affected by the extreme variates.
- As compared by mean, it is affected more by fluctuations of sampling.

The following table shows the distribution of marks of 40 students on a final examination in a college:

Marks:	60-64	55-59	50-54	45-49	40-44	35-39	30-34
No. of students:	2	4	7	5	9	7	6

Determine median of the distribution.

Mode

The mode or the modal value is the value which occurs with highest frequency. In other words, it is a value of the variable which occurs most often.

Let us suppose 12 students took a test with the scores:

32, 38, 48, 52, 52, 63, 63, 63, 72, 76, 76, 80.

Here the score 63 is one which occurs maximum number of times and thus, the value of mode in this case is 63. A distribution having one mode is called *unimodal*.

For **example**, we have scores:

32, 38, 48, 51, 52, 60, 62, 63, 72, 75, 76, 80.

What will be mode value in this score? There is no mode in this case as every score has equal frequency. Let us take another series of scores, say:

32, 38, 48, 51, 60, 62, 62, 72, 75.

We observe that there are two modes 51 and 62 as both occur twice, while others occur only once. In such a case, the distribution is called *bi-modal*. From the above discussion, it is clear that in some cases the mode may be absent, while in others there may be one or more modes.

Computation of Mode (in Ungrouped Data)

In case of ungrouped data, mode can be located simply by inspection. Here, the data are first arranged in the form of an array and then we can count the frequencies of each variate. The variate which has the maximum frequency is the mode.

Example 10:

Find the mode of the following ungrouped scores.

2, 6, 8, 9, 18, 17, 22, 22, 22, 40.

Solution:

As a first step, arrange the scores in an ascending order.

2, 6, 8, 9, 17, 18, 22, 22, 22, 40.

Since there are only 10 observations, mode can be determined by inspection only. Here variate 9th i.e. 22 has the maximum frequency 3. Therefore, 22 is the mode.

Mode in Grouped Data (Discrete Variable)

When the data is available in the form of discrete frequency distribution, a modal value is located simply by inspection.

Example 11:

Find the mode of the following frequency distribution:

Scores:	7	8	9	10	11	12
No. of students:	2	1	3	1	2	1

Solution:

Scores	*Frequency f*
7	2
8	1
9 – Mode	3 – Max. frequency
10	1
11	2
12	1

Here the variate 9 has the maximum frequency which can be determined by inspection only. Therefore, 9 is the mode of the given frequency distribution.

Mode in Grouped Data (Continuous Variable)

In the case of continuous frequency distribution, frequencies are given in various classes. Now, a class having maximum frequency is called the modal class. The precise value of mode is then determined within this modal class by using the following formula:

$$\text{Mode} = l + \frac{fm - f_1}{2fm - f_1 - f_2} \times i$$

where, l = the lower limit of the modal class.
fm = frequency of the modal class.
f_1 = frequency of the class preceding modal class.
f_2 = frequency of the class succeeding modal class.
i = class interval of the modal class.

While using the above formula for calculating mode, it is necessary that class intervals are uniformly taken in the formation of frequency distribution. Computation of mode for a continuous frequency distribution is clarified in the following Example.

Example 12:

Find mode of the following frequency distribution.

Scores:	45 – 49	40 – 44	35 – 39	30 – 34	25 – 29	20 – 24	15 –19
No. of students:	2	3	5	9	6	4	1

Solution:

Scores *Class Interval*	*Frequency* *f*
45—49	2
40—44	3
35—39	$5 - f_1$
30—34	$9 - fm$ (Modal Class)
25—29	$6 - f_2$
20—24	4
15—19	1

Here 30–34 is the modal class having maximum frequency 9. The true limits of the class are 29.5 – 34.5 (Already discussed in Section 8.3). Also the frequency of the modal class $fm = 9$ and that of preceding and succeeding classes are $f_1 = 5$ and $f_2 = 6$ respectively. Class interval $i = 5$. Now, the precise value of mode is obtained by putting these values in the following formula:

$$\text{Mode} = l + \frac{fm - f_1}{2fm - f_1 - f_2} \times i$$

$$= 29.5 + \frac{9-5}{2(9)-5-6} \times 5$$

$$= 29.5 + \frac{4}{18-11} \times 5$$

$$= 29.5 + \frac{4}{7} \times 5$$

$$= 29.5 + \frac{20}{7}$$

$$= 29.5 + 2.86$$

$$= 32.36$$

Hence, Mode = 32.36

Mode can also be calculated by another methods:

Mode = 3 Median – 2 Mean.

Example 13:

Find mode of the following frequency distribution:

Marks:	20–21	18–19	16–17	14–15	12–13	10–11	8–9
No. of students:	1	3	4	5	3	3	1

Solution:

For calculating mode by this method, we first calculate mean and median.

Class Interval	*x*	*f*	*d*	*fd*	*"Less than" Cumulative frequency C*
20—21	20.5	1	3	3	20
18—19	18.5	3	2	6	19
16—17	16.5	4	1	4	16
14—15	14.5	5	0	0	12
12—13	12.5	3	– 1	– 3	7
10—11	10.5	3	– 2	– 6	4
8—9	8.5	1	– 3	– 3	1
		N = 20	$\Sigma fd = 1$		

Mean $= a + \frac{\Sigma fd}{N} \times i$

$= 14.5 + \frac{1}{20} \times 2$

$= 14.5 + \frac{1}{10}$

$= 14.5 + 1$

$= 14.6$

Mean $= 14.6$

Since $\frac{N}{2} = \frac{20}{2} = 10$ lies in class interval 14 – 15, Median class is 14 – 15.

Median $= L + \frac{\frac{N}{2} - C}{f} \times i$

$= 13.5 + \frac{\frac{20}{2} - 7}{5} \times 2$

$= 13.5 + \frac{10 - 7}{5} \times 2$

$= 13.5 + \frac{3}{5} \times 2$

$= 13.5 + 1.2$

$= 14.7$

Median $= 14.7$

Mode = 3 Median – 2 Mean

$= 3 \times 14.7 - 2 \times 14.6$

$= 44.1 - 29.2$

$= 14.9$

Mode $= 14.9$

Merits and Demerits of Mode

Merits and Demerits of Mode following are:

- It is not well defined.
- It can be easily understood.
- Its computation is not based on all the variates.
- It is also not capable of being handled algebraically because its value is not based on all the observations.
- It is not affected by extreme variates provided they do not belong to modal class.
- As compared to mean, it is very much affected by fluctuations of sampling.

Characteristics for an Ideal Measure of Central Value

Characteristics for an ideal measure of Central Value following are:

- It should be easily defined and easily understandable.
- Its calculation should be based on all the observations.
- It should be capable for further algebraic treatment.
- It should not be affected much by the extreme values of the variable.
- It should be least affected by fluctuations of sampling.

(*i*) Using the distribution of scores that appear below, find the mode:

21, 21, 18, 18, 18, 15, 14, 12, 10, 7

(*a*) 16.5
(*b*) 15.4
(*c*) 18
(*d*) 19.35

(*ii*) Find mode by using formula

Mode = 3 Median –2 Mean, for the following frequency distribution:

Scores:	65—69	60—64	55—59	50—54	45—49	40—44	35—39
f:	1	3	4	7	9	11	8

Scores:	30—34	25—29	20—24
f:	4	2	1

(*iii*) Calculate mode by using formula

Mode = $L+\dfrac{fm-f_1}{2fm-f_1-f_2}\times i$ for the following distribution.

Scores:	20–29	30–39	40–49	50–59	60–69	70–79	80–89
f:	4	6	8	12	9	7	4

The word statistics refers to numerical facts, methodology of dealing with numerical facts or summarised figures. However, as a subject, statistics refers to that branch of knowledge which helps in the scientific collection, presentation, analysis and interpretation of numerical facts. Tests, experiments and survey studies provide us valuable data mostly in the shape of numerical scores.

Then data have to be arranged in the form of frequency distribution. The Arithmetic mean, median and mode are known as the most common measures of central tendency. A measure of central tendency is a sort of average or typical value of the item in the series. Each of these measures of the central tendency provides us single value to represent the characteristics of the whole group in its own way.

Exercises

1. (*i*)

Class Interval c.i.	*Tally* T	*Frequency* f
72—74	III	3
69—71	IIII	4
66—68	II	2
63—65	III	3
60—62	III	3
57—59	IIII	4
54—56	IIII	4
51—53	II	2
48—50	I	1
45—47	III	3
42—44	III	3
39—41	III	3

2. (*i*) **d.**

(*ii*)

Class Interval	*x*	*f*	*d*	*fd*	
72—74	73	3	5	15	
69—71	70	4	4	16	
66—68	67	2	3	6	+46
63—65	64	3	2	6	
60—62	61	3	1	3	
57—59	58	4	0	0	
54—56	55	4	–1	– 4	
51—53	52	2	–2	– 4	
48—50	49	1	–3	– 3	– 56
45—47	46	3	–4	–12	
42—44	43	3	–5	– 5	
39—41	40	3	–6	–18	
				fd = – 10	

$$X = a + \frac{\Sigma fd}{N} \times i$$

$$= 58 + \frac{-10}{35} \times 3$$

$$= 58 + \frac{(-30)}{35}$$

$$= 58 - \frac{6}{7}$$

$$= 58 - 0.86$$

$$= 57.14$$

Mean = 57.14

(*iii*) Here, we are given that

$N_1 = 32 \qquad \bar{X}_1 = 24$

$N_2 = 54 \qquad \bar{X}_2 = 31$

$N_3 = 16 \qquad \bar{X}_3 = 35$

$$X_{123} = \frac{N_1\bar{x}_1 + N_2\bar{x}_2 + N_3\bar{x}_3}{N_1 + N_2 + N_3}$$

$$= \frac{32 \times 24 + 54 \times 31 + 16 \times 35}{32 + 54 + 16}$$

$$= \frac{768 + 1674 + 560}{102}$$

$$= \frac{3002}{102}$$

$$= 29.43$$

$$\bar{x}_{123} = 29.43$$

3. (*i*)

Marks	*No. of Students* *f*	*'Less than' Cumulative frequency C*
60—64	2	40
55—59	4	38
50—54	7	34
45—49	5	27
40—44	9	22
35—39	7	13
30—34	6	6
	N = 40	

$$\text{Median} = L + \frac{\frac{N}{2} - C}{f} \times i$$

$$= 39.5 + \frac{\frac{40}{2} - 13}{9} \times 5$$

$$= 39.5 + \frac{20 - 13}{9} \times 5$$

$$= 39.5 + \frac{7}{5} \times 5$$

$$= 39.5 + \frac{35}{9}$$

$$= 39.5 + 3.89$$

$$= - 43.39$$

$$\text{Median} = 43.39$$

4. (*i*) *a*
(*ii*) *c*
(*iii*)

Class Interval	*x*	*f*	*d*	*fd*	*'Less than' Cumulative frequency C*
65—69	67	1	+5	5	50
60—64	62	3	+4	12	49
55—59	57	4	+3	12	45
50—54	52	7	+2	14	42
45—49	47	9	+1	9	35
40—44	42	11	0	0	26
35—39	37	8	1	–8	15
30—34	32	4	2	–8	7
25—29	27	2	–3	–6	3
20—24	22	1	–4	–4	1
		N = 50		Σ*fd* = 26	

$$\bar{X} = a + \frac{\Sigma fd}{N} \times i$$

$$= 42 + \frac{26}{50} \times 5$$

$$= 42 + \frac{26}{10}$$

$$= 42 + 2.6$$

$$= 44.6$$

Mean = 44.6

Since N/2 = $\frac{50}{2}$ = 25, it lies in class interval 40 – 44, the median class is 40 – 44.

$$\text{Median} = L + \frac{\frac{N}{2} - C}{f} \times i$$

$$= 39.5 + \frac{\frac{50}{2} - 15}{11} \times 5$$

$$= 39.5 + \frac{25-15}{11} \times 5$$

$$= 39.5 + \frac{10}{11} \times 5$$

$$= 39.5 + \frac{50}{11}$$

$$= 39.5 + 4.55$$

$$= 44.05$$

Median = 44.5

Mode = 3 Median – 2 Mean.

Here we know Median = 44.05, Mean = 44.6

By putting these values

$$= 3 \times 44.05 - 2 \times 44.6$$

$$= 132.15 - 89.2$$

$$= 42.95$$

Mode = 42.95

5.

Class Interval	*f*
20—29	4
30—39	6
40—49	8–f_1
50—59	12 – fm (Modal Class)
60—69	9 – f_2
70—79	7
80—89	4

$$\text{Mode} = l + \frac{fm - f_1}{2fm - f_1 - f_2} \times i$$

$$= 49.5 + \frac{12-8}{2 \times 12 - 8 - 9}$$

$$= 49.5 + \frac{4}{7} \times 10$$

$$= 49.5 + \frac{40}{7}$$

$$= 49.5 + 5.71$$

$$= 55.21$$

Mode = 55.21

2

Measures of Dispersion Percentile

We discussed the commonly used measures of central tendency which are useful in providing descriptive information concerning a set of data. However, the information so obtained is neither exhaustive nor comprehensive, as the mean does not lead us to know whether the observations are close to each other or far apart. Median is the positional average and has nothing to do with the variability of the observations in the series. Mode is the largest occurring value independent of other values of the set.

This leads us to conclude that a central value or an average alone cannot describe the distribution adequately. Moreover, two or more sets may have the same mean but they may be quite different. To clear this point, let us consider the scores of two groups of students on the same test:

Scores of 1st Group:	45,	57,	24,	41,	68,	84,	55,	62,	90,	74.
Scores of 2nd Group:	57,	60,	63,	68,	70,	52,	50.			

Here, both the groups have the same mean score of 60. From first inspection, we might say that the two sets of scores are equal in nature. In the first group, the range of scores is from 24 to 90, while in the second, range is from 50 to 70. This difference in range shows that the students in the second group are more homogeneous in scoring than those in the first. So both the groups differ widely in the variability of scores.

Thus, while studying a distribution it is equally important to know whether the observations are clustered around or scattered away from the point of central tendency. Measures of dispersion help us in studying the extent to which observations are scattered about the average or the central value.

Measures of Dispersion

Measures of Dispersions following are:

- Range
- Quartile Deviation (Q)

- Mean Deviation (M.D.)
- Variance and Standard Deviation (S.D.)
- Combined Variance and Standard Deviation
- Coefficient of Variation
- When to use various Measures of Dispersion.

Range

The range of a set of observations is defined as the difference between the largest and the smallest value. The range is a measure of observations among themselves and does not give an idea about the spread of the observations around some central value. The range is defined by $R = X_L - X_s$

where, X_L = The largest of the observed values.

X_s = The smallest of the observed values.

Example 1:

Calculate Range of the following set of scores:

28, 21, 41, 30, 33, 37, 19, 27.

Solution:

Here, the *largest* observed Score $X_L = 41$.

The *smallest* observed Score $X_S = 19$.

Therefore, Range (R) $= X_L - X_S$

$= 41 - 19$

$R = 21$

Exercise

1. Calculate Range for the following set of scores:
   18, 40, 42, 46, 35, 25, 23, 27, 17, 37.

QUARTILE DEVIATION (Q)

The quartile deviation is defined as the difference between Q_3 and Q_1 in a frequency distribution. It is computed by the formula:

$$Q = \frac{Q_3 - Q_1}{2}$$

where, Q = Quartile Deviation.

Q_3 = Third Quartile.

Q_1 = First Quartile.

For computing Q, we must first get the values of Q_1 and Q_3 — the first and third quartiles.

Quartiles

In the previous Chapter, we discussed about median as a measure of central tendency. We know that median is the value of the score which divides the distribution into two equal halves. Similarly, quartiles are the points which divide a distribution into quarters. Q_1 is the first quartile, Q_3 is the third quartile and Q_2 is the second quartile or median.

The quartile can be computed by the following formula:

$$Q_1 = L + \frac{\frac{N}{4} - Cf}{f} \times i$$

$$Q_3 = L + \frac{\frac{3N}{4} - Cf}{f}$$

where, L = lower limit of the class in which quartile lies.

Cf = 'less than' cumulative frequency of the class preceding to quartile class.

f = frequency of the quartile class.

i = size of class interval.

To find Q_1 and Q_3, we first find Quartile Class.

The quartile class for Q_1 is the class in which N/4th case falls. Similarly for Q_3, quartile class is the class in which 3N/4th case falls. The computation of Q_1 and Q_3 may be explained through the following example:

Example 2:

Calculate first and third quartile for the following frequency distribution:

Scores:	14–15,	12–13,	10–11,	8–9,	6–7,	4–5
f:	3	8	15	20	10	4

Solution:

Scores Class Interval c.i.	*Frequency f*	*'Less than' Cumulative frequency Cf*
14—15	3	60
12—13	8	57
10—11	15	49
8—9	20	34
6—7	10	14
4—5	4	4
	N = 60	

Calculations of Q_1: Since $\frac{N}{2} = \frac{60}{2}$ = 15th cases fall in the class interval 8–9; the quartile class for Q_1 is 8–9, with its class interval 2 and true limits '7.5–9.5'.

Therefore, $L = 7.5$, $Cf = 14$, $f = 20$, $i = 2$,

$$\frac{N}{4} = 15$$

Putting these values in the formula, we have

$$Q_1 = L + \frac{\frac{N}{4} - Cf}{f} \times i$$

$$= 7.5 + \frac{15 - 14}{20} \times 2$$

$$= 7.5 + \frac{1}{20} \times 2$$

$$= 7.5 + 0.1$$

$$= 7.6$$

$$Q_1 = 7.9$$

Calculation of Q_3: Since $\frac{3N}{4} = \frac{3 \times 60}{4}$ 45th cases fall in the class interval 10–11, the quartile class for Q_3 is 10 –11 with its class interval 2 and true limits '9.5–11.15'.

Therefore, $L = 9.5$, $Cf = 34$, $f = 15$, $i = 2$.

$$\frac{3N}{4} = 45$$

Putting these values in the formula, we have

$$Q_3 = L + \frac{\frac{3N}{4} - Cf}{f} \times i$$

$$= 9.5 + \frac{45 - 34}{15} \times 2$$

$$= 9.5 + \frac{11}{15} \times 2$$

$$= 9.5 + \frac{22}{15}$$

$$= 9.5 + 1.467$$
$$= 10.967$$
$$Q_3 = 10.967$$

Example 3:

Find Quartile deviation for the frequency distribution given in Example 2.

Solution:

Quartile deviation is computed by the formula:

$$Q = \frac{Q_3 - Q_1}{2}$$

As calculated in Example 2

$$Q_3 = 10.967$$
$$Q_1 = 7.6$$

$$\text{Hence, } Q = \frac{10.967 - 7.6}{2}$$
$$= \frac{3.367}{2}$$
$$= 1.683$$
$$Q = 1.683$$

Exercises

1. What is the value of Q when $Q_1 = 34$ and $Q_3 = 76$?
   (*a*) 21 (*b*) 42 (*c*) 110
   (*d*) More information is needed to determine the answer.
2. The following is the data given in the form of frequency distribution:

Scores	*f*
90—99	2
80—89	12
70—79	22
60—69	20
50—59	14
40—49	4
30—39	1
	N = 75

   (*a*) Calculate first and third Quartiles i.e. Q_1 and Q_3.
   (*b*) Calculate Quartile Deviation (Q.D.).

MEAN DEVIATION (MD)

The average of the absolute deviations of every variate value from the mean is called the Mean Deviation (MD) or the Average Deviation (AD). In averaging deviations to find the mean deviation, no account is taken of signs, and all deviations whether plus or minus are treated as per positive. Thus, if some of the deviations are +4, –9, +2, +5, –1 and –3, we simply add 4, 9, 2, 5, 1 and 3 getting 24.

Computation of Mean Deviation From Ungrouped Data:

The formula for computing mean deviation from ungrouped data is

$$MD = \frac{\Sigma[X - \bar{X}]}{N}$$

where, N = the number of observations and $\Sigma[X - \bar{X}]$ signifies the sum of absolute deviations (irrespective of +ve or –ve sign) taken from the mean of the series.

The computation of mean deviation will be more clear by taking an example.

Example 4:

Find mean deviation for the following set of observations:

X = 55, 45, 63, 76, 67, 84

Solution:

In order to find mean deviation, we first calculate mean for the given set of observations.

S. No.	*X*	*Deviation from Mean* $x = (X - \bar{X})$	*Absolute deviations* (sign Ignored) $[X - \bar{X}]$
1	55	–10	10
2	45	–20	20
3	63	–2	2
4	76	+11	11
5	67	+2	2
6	84	+19	19
N = 6	ΣX = 390		$\Sigma[X - \bar{X}] = 64$

Here, Mean $= \frac{\Sigma X}{N}$ (Already discussed in the previous Chapter).

$$= \frac{390}{6}$$

$$\bar{X} = 65$$

Formula for computing the mean deviation is:

$$MD = \frac{\Sigma[X - \bar{X}]}{N}$$

$$= \frac{64}{6} = 10.67$$

$$MD = 10.67$$

Mean Deviation from Grouped Data

In case of grouped data, the formula for calculating the mean deviation is as follows:

$$MD = \frac{\Sigma[X - \bar{X}]}{N}$$

Computation of mean deviation will be clear from the following example:

Example 5:

Find mean deviation for the following frequency distribution:

Scores:	14—15,	12—13,	10—11,	8—9,	6—7,	4—5
f:	3	8	15	20	10	4

Solution:

As usual, mean for the given distribution is first calculated to get the mean deviation.

Scores classes	*f*	X	*f*X	$[X - \bar{X}]$ $[X - 9.231]$	$f[X - \bar{X}]$
14—15	3	14.5	43.5	5.27	15.87
12—13	8	12.5	100.0	3.27	26.16
10—11	15	10.5	157.5	1.27	19.05
8—9	20	8.5	170.0	0.73	14.6
6—7	10	6.5	65.0	2.73	27.3
4—5	4	4.5	18.0	4.73	18.92
	N = 60	$\Sigma fx = 554$		$\Sigma f[X - \bar{X}]$	= 121.84

$$\text{Here, Mean} = \frac{\Sigma fX}{N}$$

$$\bar{X} = \frac{554}{60} = 9.23$$

Mean = 9.23

$$\text{MD} = \frac{\Sigma f\left[X - \bar{X}\right]}{N}$$

$$= \frac{121.84}{60} = 2.03$$

MD = 2.03.

Exercise

1. Find the mean deviation for the following frequency distribution:

Scores	*No. of Students*
60—62	5
63—65	18
66—68	42
69—71	27
72—74	8

VARIANCE AND STANDARD DEVIATION (SD)

The most widely used measures for showing the variability of a set of scores are Variance and Standard Deviation (SD). The variance is defined as the average of the squares of deviations of the observations from the arithmetic mean. The standard deviation is defined as the positive square root of the arithmetic mean of the squares of deviations of the observations from the arithmetic mean. It may also be called as 'Root mean square deviation from mean' and is generally denoted by the small Greek letter (Sigma).

Computation of Variance and Standard Deviation for Ungrouped Data

There are two ways of computing variance and Standard Deviation (SD) for ungrouped data:

- Direct Method
- Short-cut Method

Direct Method

The formulas for finding the variance and SD for a set of scores are as follows:

$$\text{Variance } \sigma^2 = \frac{\sum(X-\bar{X})^2}{N}$$

$$SD(\sigma^2) = \sqrt{\frac{\sum(X-\bar{X})^2}{N}}$$

X = Individual Score

$\bar{X}$ = The Arithmetic Mean

N = Total Number of observations.

The steps involved in the computation procedure may be listed as:

- Calculate the arithmetic mean $\bar{X}$ of the given data.
- Obtain deviation of each variate from $\bar{X}$ as $(X-\bar{X})$.
- Square each deviation to get $(X-\bar{X})^2$.
- Obtain the sum of squared deviations as $\sum(X-\bar{X})^2$.
- Using formula, calculate variance □ σ^2 as the arithmetic mean of the squared deviations, i.e.

$$\sigma^2 = \frac{\sum(X-\bar{X})^2}{N}$$

- The positive square root of variance is then calculated to get SD as:

$$\sigma = \sqrt{\frac{\sum(X-\bar{X})^2}{N}}$$

The following example will show how these steps are followed:

Example 6:

Find the variance and SD for the following ungrouped data:

23, 21, 18, 17, 16, 15, 14, 12.

Solution:

S. No.	X	$X-\bar{X}$	$(X-\bar{X})^2$
1	23	6	36
2	21	4	16
3	18	1	1
4	17	0	0
5	16	−1	1
6	15	−2	4
7	14	−3	9
8	12	4	16
$N = 8$	$\Sigma X = 136$		$\Sigma(X-\bar{X})^2 = 92$

$$\bar{X} = \frac{\sum X}{N}$$

$$= \frac{136}{8} = 17$$

$$\sigma^2 = \frac{\sum(X-\bar{x})}{N}$$

$$= \frac{92}{8} = 11.5$$

$$\sigma^2 = 11.5$$

$$\sigma = \sqrt{\frac{\left(\sum X-\bar{x}\right)^2}{N}}$$

$$= \frac{92}{8}$$

$$= 11.5$$

where $\sum X^2$ = the sum of squares of raw scores.

$\bar{X}^2$ = the square of arithmetic mean of the given data.

N = total number of observations.

The following steps are involved in the computation procedure of variance and SD:

- Calculate the arithmetic mean $\bar{X}$ of the given data.
- Square of each raw score to obtain x^2.

- Sum of squares to get $\sum x^2$.
- Use the formula to obtain variance i.e.

$$\sigma^2 = \frac{\sum x^2}{N} - \overline{x}^2$$

- The positive square root of variance is then calculated to get SD

$$\sigma = \sqrt{\frac{\sum X^2 - \overline{x}^2}{N}}$$

These steps will clear from the following example:

Example 7:

Find the variance and SD for the data given in Example 6 through 'raw score' formula.

Solution:

S. No.	X	X^2
1	23	529
2	21	441
3	18	324
4	17	289
5	16	256
6	15	225
7	14	196
8	12	144
N = 8	$\Sigma X = 136$	$\Sigma X^2 = 2{,}404$

$$\overline{X} = \frac{\sum X}{N}$$

$$= \frac{136}{8} = 17$$

Substitute the values in the formula

$$\sigma^2 = \frac{\sum X^2}{N} - \overline{x}^2$$

$$= \frac{2404}{8} - (17)^2$$

$$= 300.5 - 289 = 11.5$$

$$\sigma^2 = 11.5$$

$$\sigma = \sqrt{\frac{\sum X^2}{N} - \bar{x}^2}$$

$$\sigma = \sqrt{\frac{2404}{8} - (17)^2}$$

$$= \sqrt{300.5 - 289}$$

$$= \sqrt{11.5} = 3.39$$

$$\sigma = 3.39$$

Short-cut Method

In most of the cases, the arithmetic mean of the given data happens to be a fractional value and then the process of taking deviations and squaring them becomes tedious and time-consuming in the computation of variance and SD. To facilitate computation in such situations, the deviations may be taken from an assumed mean. The short-cut formula for calculating SD will then becomes:

$$\text{Variance} = \sigma^2 = \frac{\sum d^2}{N} - \left(\frac{\sum d}{N}\right)^2$$

$$\text{and SD} = \sqrt{\frac{\sum d^2}{N} - \left(\frac{\sum d}{N}\right)^2}$$

where, d = deviation of the variate from an assumed mean, say 'a' i.e., $d = (x - a)$.

d^2 = the square of the deviations.

Σd = the sum of the deviations.

Σd^2 = the sum of the squared deviations.

N = the total number of variates.

The following are the steps of this methods for calculating variance and SD:

Take some assumed mean, say 'a' (as in the case of calculating arithmetic mean):

- Find deviation from '*a*' for each score to obtain $d = x - a$.
- Sum all d to obtain Σd.
- Square each deviation d to obtain d^2.
- Sum all d^2 to obtain Σd^2.
- Use formula to obtain variance i.e.

$$\sigma^2 = \frac{\sum d^2}{N} - \left(\frac{\sum d}{N}\right)^2$$

- The positive square root of variance is then calculated to get SD i.e.

$$\sigma = \sqrt{\frac{\sum d^2}{N} - \left(\frac{\sum d}{N}\right)^2}$$

The computation procedure is clarified in the following example:

Example 8:

Find the variance and SD by short-cut method for the data given in Example 6.

Solution:

S. No.	*x*	*d = x − a* *a = 18*	*d*²
1	23	+5	25
2	21	+3	9
3	18	0	0
4	17	1	1
5	16	−2	4
6	15	−3	9
7	14	−4	16
8	12	6	36
N = 8		$\Sigma d = 8$	$\Sigma d^2 = 100$

Let us take assumed mean = 18

(we can take other values also as assumed mean)

Therefore, $\Sigma d = 8$, $\Sigma d^2 = 100$, N = 8

$$\sigma^2 = \frac{\sum d^2}{N} - \left(\frac{\sum d}{N}\right)^2$$

$$= \frac{100}{8} - \left(\frac{8}{8}\right)^2$$

$$= 12.5 - 1 = 11.5$$

$$\text{Variance} = 11.5$$

$$\sigma = \sqrt{\frac{\sum d^2}{N} - \left(\frac{\sum d}{N}\right)^2}$$

$$= \sqrt{\frac{100}{8} - \left(\frac{8}{8}\right)^2}$$

$$= \sqrt{12.5 - 1}$$

$$= \sqrt{11.5} = 3.39$$

$$SD = 3.39$$

From examples (7) and (8) what we found. We found that variance (11.5) and SD (3.39) are the same in both i.e. Raw Score and Short-cut method.

Computation of Variance and Standard Deviation for Grouped Data

For circulating variance and Standard Deviation (SD) for grouped data, there are two methods analogue to ungrouped data:

- Direct Method.
- Short-cut Method.

Direct Method

This method uses actual arithmetic mean in considering deviations of given observations. The formulas for calculating variance and SD are as follows:

$$\text{Variance} = \sigma^2 = \frac{\sum f(X - \bar{x})^2}{N}$$

$$SD = \sigma = \sqrt{\frac{\sum f(X - \bar{x})^2}{N}}$$

The method can be described by the following steps:

- Find the mid-value of all the classes to obtain x.
- Calculate the arithmetic mean $\overline{x}$ of the given data by the formula $\overline{X} = \frac{\Sigma fx}{N}$.
- Take deviation from mean $\overline{x}$ of each variate to obtain $X - \overline{x}$.
- Take square of each $(X-\overline{x})$ and then multiply with corresponding frequency to get $f(X-\overline{x})^2$.
- Sum all $f(X-\overline{x})^2$ to get $\Sigma f(X-\overline{x})^2$.
- Use the above formulas to obtain variance and SD.

The computation procedure will be clarified in the following example:

Example 9:

Find the variance and SD for the following frequency distribution.

Class interval:	80—84	75—79	70—74	65—69	60—64	55—59
f:	1	2	4	3	6	5

Class interval:	50—54	45—49	40—44	35—39	30—34	25—29
f:	3	5	3	5	1	2

Solution:

Class interval	f	x	fx	$(X-\overline{x})$	$(X-\overline{x})^2$	$f(X-\overline{x})^2$
80—84	1	82	82	27.75	770.06	770.60
75—79	2	77	154	22.75	517.56	1,035.12
70—74	4	72	288	17.75	315.06	1,260.24
65—69	3	67	201	12.75	162.56	487.68
60—64	6	62	372	7.75	60.06	360.36
55—59	5	57	285	2.75	7.56	37.80
50—54	3	52	156	–2.25	5.06	15.18
45—49	5	47	235	–7.25	52.56	262.80
40—44	3	42	126	–12.25	150.06	450.18
35—39	5	37	185	–17.25	297.56	1,487.80
30—34	1	32	32	–22.25	495.06	495.06
25—29	2	27	54	–27.25	742.56	1,485.12
	N = 40		2.170			$\Sigma f(X-\overline{x})^2$ = 8,147.40

$$\text{Mean} = \frac{\sum fx}{N}$$

$$= \frac{2170}{40} = 54.25$$

$$\overline{x} = 54.25$$

$$\text{Variance} = \frac{\sum f(X-\overline{x})}{N}$$

$$= \frac{8,147.40}{40} = 203.69$$

$$\sigma^2 = 203.69$$

$$\text{SD} = \sqrt{\frac{\sum f(X-\overline{x})^2}{N}}$$

$$= \sqrt{\frac{8,147.40}{40}}$$

$$= \sqrt{203.69} = 14.3$$

$$\sigma = 14.3$$

The method illustrated above is quite tedious. Let us consider the 'raw-score' formula for grouped data to compute variance and SD as already discussed for ungrouped data. The 'raw-score' formula is:

$$\text{Variance} = \frac{\sum fX^2}{N} - X^2$$

$$\text{SD} = \sqrt{\frac{\sum fX^2}{N} - \overline{x}^2}$$

The steps involved in the computation procedure may be listed as:

- Find the mid-value X of all the classes.
- Multiply each X by corresponding frequency to obtain fX and

- Calculate mean by the formula

$$\bar{X} = \frac{\sum fX}{N}$$

- Take square of each X and multiply by corresponding frequency to obtain fX^2.
- Sum all fX^2 to obtain ΣfX^2.
- Use the above formulas to obtain variance and standard deviation.

The following example will clear these steps:

Example 10:

Find the variance and SD for the frequency distribution given in Example 9 through 'raw-score' formula.

Class interval	*f*	X	*fX*	X^2	fX^2
80—84	1	82	82	6,724	6,724
75—79	2	77	154	5,929	11,858
70—74	4	72	288	5,184	20,736
65—69	3	67	201	4,489	13,467
60—64	6	62	372	3,844	23,064
55—59	5	57	285	3,249	16,245
50—54	3	52	156	2,704	8,112
45—49	5	47	235	2,209	11,045
40—44	3	42	126	1,764	5,292
35—39	5	37	185	1,369	6,845
30—34	1	32	32	1,024	1,024
25—29	2	27	54	729	1,458
	N = 40		ΣfX = 2,170		ΣfX^2 = 1,25,870

$$\text{Mean} = \frac{\sum fX}{N}$$

$$= \frac{2170}{40} = 54.25$$

$$\bar{x} = 54.25$$

$$\text{Variance} = \frac{\sum fX^2}{N} - \bar{x}^2$$

$$= \frac{1,25,870}{40} - (54.25)^2$$

$$= 3,146.75 - 2,943.06 = 203.69$$

$$\text{Variance} = 203.69$$

$$\text{SD} = \sqrt{\frac{\sum fX^2}{N} - \bar{x}^2}$$

$$= \sqrt{\frac{1,25,870}{40} - (54.25)^2}$$

$$= \sqrt{3,146.75 - 2,943.06}$$

$$= \sqrt{203.69} = 14.3$$

$$\text{SD} = 14.3$$

Variance (203.69) and SD (14.3) are the same as in the previous example.

Short-cut Method

In short-cut method, our main aim is to reduce the computations. To simplify the procedure, we take deviations from some assumed mean instead of actual mean. Calculations can be further simplified by dividing these deviations from class interval. The formulas for calculating variance and SD by this method are:

$$\text{Variance} = i^2\left[\frac{\sum fd^2}{N} - \left(\frac{\sum fd}{N}\right)^2\right]$$

$$\text{SD} = i\sqrt{\left[\frac{\sum fd^2}{N} - \left(\frac{\sum fd}{N}\right)^2\right]}$$

where, d = deviation from assumed mean i.e. $\frac{x-a}{i}$

N = total number of observations.

i = class interval.

Computation by this method can be described by the following steps:

- Take mid-value of each class to obtain x.
- Take some assumed mean say 'a' near the centre of the distribution.
- Subtract 'a' from x and divide by i to obtain d.
- Multiply each d by corresponding frequency to get fd.
- Take square of each d and multiply by corresponding frequency to obtain fd^2.
- Sum all fd and fd^2 to get Σfd and Σfd^2.

Use the above formula to calculate variance and SD. The following example will illustrate how these steps are followed:

Example 11:

Use short-cut method to compute variance and SD for the frequency distribution given in Example 9.

Solution:

First, in the middle of the distribution choose an estimated mean class. We choose 50–54 class. However, other classes can also be chosen. The mid-point of this class is 52, which will be assumed mean 'a'.

Class Interval c.i.	f	X	$d = \frac{X - a}{i}$ $d = \frac{X - 52}{5}$	fd	fd^2
80—84	1	82	6	6	36
75—79	2	77	5	10	50
70—74	4	72	4	16	64
65—69	3	67	3	9	27
60—64	6	62	2	12	24
55—59	5	57	1	5	5
50—54	3	52	0	0	0
45—49	5	47	– 1	– 5	5
40—44	3	42	– 2	– 6	12
35—39	5	37	– 3	– 15	45
30—34	1	32	– 4	– 4	16
25—29	2	27	– 5	– 10	50
	N = 40			$\Sigma fd = 18$	$\Sigma fd^2 = 334$

Here, $\Sigma fd^2 = 334$, $\Sigma fd = 18$, N = 40

Putting these values in the formula:

$$\text{Variance} = i^2\left[\frac{\Sigma fd^2}{N} - \left(\frac{\Sigma fd}{N}\right)^2\right]$$

$$= (5)^2 \times \left[\frac{334}{40} - \left(\frac{18}{40}\right)^2\right]$$

$$= 25\ [8.35 - 0.2025]$$

$$= 25 \times 8.1475$$

$$= 203.69$$

Variance = 203.69

$$\text{SD} = i\sqrt{\left[\frac{\Sigma fd^2}{N} - \left(\frac{\Sigma fd}{N}\right)^2\right]}$$

$$= 5\sqrt{\frac{334}{40} - \left[\frac{18}{40}\right]^2}$$

$$= 5\sqrt{8.35 - .2025}$$

$$= 5\sqrt{8.1475}$$

$$= 5 \times 2.85$$

$$= 14.3$$

$$\text{SD} = 14.3$$

What does this illustration show?

This illustrates that the short-cut method reduces the calculations.

Exercises

1. The variance of a distribution is 9. What will be the Standard Deviation?
   (*a*) 4.5
   (*b*) 3
   (*c*) 81
   (*d*) None of these.
2. For the following list of test scores:
   52, 50, 56, 68, 65, 62, 57, 70
   (*a*) Calculate mean, SD and Variance by direct method.

(*b*) Calculate SD and Variance by using 'raw-score' formula.
(*c*) Calculate SD and Variance by short-cut method.

3. The following is the data given in the form of frequency distribution:

Scores	*f*
60—69	1
50—59	4
40—49	10
30—39	15
20—29	8
10—19	2

(*a*) Calculate mean, SD and Variance by direct method.
(*b*) Calculate SD and Variance by using 'raw-score' formula.
(*c*) Calculate Variance and SD by using short-cut method.

COMBINED VARIANCE AND STANDARD DEVIATION

If two frequency distributions have means $\overline{x}_1$ and $\overline{x}_2$ and standard deviations σ_1 and σ_2 respectively, then the combined variance, denoted by σ_{12}^2 and SD, denoted by σ_{12} of the two distributions is obtained by using:

$$\sigma_{12}^2 = \frac{N_1\left(\sigma_1^2 + D_1^2\right) + N_2\left(\sigma_2^2 + D_2^2\right)}{N_1 + N_2}$$

$$\sigma_{12} = \sqrt{\frac{N_1\left(\sigma_1^2 + D_1^2\right) + N_2\left(\sigma_2^2 + D_2^2\right)}{N_1 + N_2}}$$

where,

N_1 = total number of observations in first frequency distribution.
N_2 = total number of observations in second frequency distribution.
σ_1 = SD of the first frequency distribution.
σ_2 = SD of the second frequency distribution.
$D_1 = \left(\overline{X}_2 - \overline{x}_1\right)$ = the difference between the combined mean and the mean of the first frequency distribution.
$D_2 = \left(\overline{X}_{12} - \overline{x}_1\right)$ = the difference between combined mean and the mean of the second frequency distribution.

The formula can be extended to any number of observations. An example will illustrate the use of the formula.

Example 12:

Suppose we are given the means and SD's on an achievement test for two classes differing in size, and we are asked to find the variance and SD of the combined group data are as follows:

	N	$\overline{x}$	SD
Class A:	25	80	15
Class B:	75	70	25

Solution:

First, by using the following formula, the combined mean score will be:

$$X_{12} = \frac{N_1\overline{x}_1 + N_2\overline{x}_2}{N_1 + N_2}$$

$$= \frac{25 \times 80 + 75 \times 70}{25 + 75}$$

$$= \frac{2000 + 5250}{100}$$

$$= \frac{7250}{100} = 72.50$$

Therefore, $D_1 = (\overline{x}_{12} - \overline{x}_1) = 72.5 - 80 = -7.5$

$D_2 = (\overline{x}_{12} - \overline{x}_2) = 72.5 - 70 = 2.5$

Now, by substituting the values in the following formula:

$$\sigma^2_{12} = \frac{N_1(\sigma_1^2 + D_1^2) + N_2(\sigma_2^2 + D_2^2)}{N_1 + N_2}$$

$$= \frac{25[15^2 + (-7.5)^2] + 75[25^{-2} + (2.5)^2]}{25 + 75}$$

$$= \frac{25(225 + 56.25) + 75(625 + 6.25)}{100}$$

$$= \frac{25 \times 281.25 + 75 \times 631.25}{100}$$

$$= \frac{7031.25 + 47343.75}{100}$$

$$= \frac{54375}{100} = 543.75$$

$$= 543.75$$

$$\sigma_{12} = \sqrt{\frac{N_1\left(\sigma_1{}^2 + D_1{}^2\right) + N_2\left(\sigma_2{}^2 + D\right)^2}{N_1 + N_2}}$$

$$= \sqrt{\frac{25\left[15^2 + (-7.5)^2\right] + 75\left[25^2 + (2.5)^2\right]}{25 + 75}}$$

$$= \sqrt{\frac{25[225 + 56.251] + 75[625 + 6.25]}{100}}$$

$$= \sqrt{\frac{25 \times 281.25 + 75 \times 631.25}{100}}$$

$$= \sqrt{\frac{7031.25 + 47343.75}{100}}$$

$$= \sqrt{\frac{54375}{100}}$$

$$= \sqrt{543.75} = 23.32$$

$$\sigma_{12} = 23.32$$

In Sample A (N = 150), A $\bar{x}$ = 120 and σ = 20; in Sample B (N=75), $\bar{x}$ = 126 and σ = 22. What are the mean and SD of A and B when combined into one distribution of 225 cases?

COEFFICIENT OF VARIATION

All the measures of dispersion discussed so far have units. If two series differ in their units of measurement, their variability cannot be compared by any measures so far. Also, the size of measures of dispersion depends upon the size of values. Hence, in situations where either the two series have different units of measurements, or their means differ sufficiently in size, the coefficient of variation should be used as a measure of dispersion.

It is sometimes called the coefficient of relative variability. It is a unitless measure of dispersion and also takes into account the size of the means of the two series. It is the best measure to compare the variability of two series or sets of observations. A series with less coefficient of variation is considered more consistent.

Coefficient of variation of a series of variate values is ratio of standard deviation to the mean multiplied by 100.

It σ is the standard deviation and $\bar{x}$ is the mean of the set of values, the coefficient of variation is,

$$C.V. = \frac{\sigma}{\overline{X}} \times 100$$

An example will illustrate the use of formula.

Example 13:

From the data give in Example 9 calculate coefficient of variation.

Solution:

We have already calculated $\overline{x} = 54.25$ and SD = 14.3 from the data given in example. Therefore, by using the formula, we get

$$C.V. = \frac{\sigma}{\overline{x}} \times 100$$

$$= \frac{14.3}{54.25} \times 100$$

$$= 0.26 + 100 = 26.0$$

$$C.V. = 26.0$$

PERCENTILE

Percentile is nothing but a sort of measure used to indicate the relative position of a single item of individual in context with the group to which the item of individual belongs. In other words, it is used to tell the relative position of a given score among other scores. A percentile refers to a point in a distribution of scores or values below which a given percentage of the cases occur.

The percentile is named for the percentage of cases below it. Thus, 67 per cent of the observations are below the sixty seventh percentile, which is written as P_{67}. The middle of a distribution or a point below which 50 per cent of cases lies in the fiftieth percentile P_{50}, which is median, has been discussed in detail in the previous unit. Similarly P_{25} and P_{75} are the first quartile Q_1 and third quartile Q_3 respectively which has been previously discussed in the section.

Computation of Percentile

When we wish to compute the percentile, we will determine the score below which a given per cent of cases will fall. First the class in which the Pth percentile lies may be identified. This is the class in which PN/100th frequency falls. The formula for computing percentile is as follows:

$$P_p = L + \frac{\left\{\frac{PN}{100} - ef\right\} \times i}{f}$$

where,

L = The lower limit of the Pth percentile class.

N = Total number of cases.

Cf = Less than cumulative frequency of class preceding to percentile class.

f = Frequency of the percentile class.

i = Class interval

The computation procedure is clarified in the following example:

Example 14:

Find the 45th percentile, P_{45} for the following frequency distribution:

Class Interval:	80—84	75—79	70—74	65—69	60—64	55—59
f:	1	2	4	3	6	5

Class Interval:	50—54	45—49	40—44	35—39	30—34	25—29
f:	3	5	3	5	1	2

Solution:

Class Interval c.i.	*Frequency* f	*"Less than" Cumulative Frequency* Cf
80—84	1	40
75—79	2	39
70—74	4	37
65—69	3	33
60—64	6	30
55—59	5	24
50—54	3	19
45—49	5	16
40—44	3	11
35—39	5	8
30—34	1	3
25—29	2	2
	N = 40	

Since $\frac{PN}{100} = \frac{45 \times 40}{100}$ = 18th frequency lies in 50–54 class, hence P_{45} class is 50–54.

Therefore, actual lower limit of class is = 49.5

$Cf = 16$

$f = 3$

$i = 5$

Putting the values in the formula

$$P_{45} = L + \frac{\left\{\frac{45N}{100} - Cf\right\}}{f} \times i$$

$$= 49.5 + \frac{\left\{\frac{45 \times 40}{100} - 16\right\}}{3} \times 5$$

$$= 49.5 + \frac{18 - 16}{3} \times 5$$

$$= 49.5 + \frac{2}{3} \times 5$$

$= 49.5 + 3.3$

$= 52.8$

$P_{45} = 52.8$

In this frequency distribution, 52.8 is the point below which 45 percent of cases will fall.

PERCENTILE RANKS

The percentile rank of a given score in a distribution is the percent of the total scores which fall below the given score. A percentile rank, then indicates the position of a score in a distribution in percentile terms. If for example, a student had a score which was higher than 70 per cent of the scores in the distribution, but not higher than 71 per cent his percentile rank would be 70.

Computation of Percentile Ranks

To compute percentile rank for a score from grouped data, we will need to determine the number of cases below the score in order to determine what per cent of the total cases would fall below that score. The formula for computing percentile rank is as below:

$$Pr = \frac{100}{N}\left\{\frac{\text{raw score} - 1}{i} \times f + Cf\right\}$$

Where symbols have the same meaning as in the case of percentiles.

Let us explain this by taking an example.

Example 15:

Find percentile rank for the score of 63 in the frequency distribution given in Example 14.

Solution:

Let us consider the values that will be substituted into the formula; raw score = 63 (given in the problem).

L– 59.5 (since the score 63 falls in the class 60 – 64 for which the real lower limit is 59.5)

$$l = 5 \qquad f = 6$$

$$Cf = 24 \qquad N = 40$$

The Computation is as follows:

$$PR = \frac{100}{N}\left\{\frac{\text{raw score} - 1}{1} \times f + Cf\right\}$$

$$= \frac{100}{40}\left\{\frac{63 - 59.5}{5} \times 6 + 24\right\}$$

$$= \frac{100}{40}\left\{\frac{3.5 \times 6 + 24}{5}\right\}$$

$$= \frac{100}{40}\{4.2 + 24\}$$

$$= \frac{100}{40}(28.2)$$

$$= \frac{2820}{40}$$

$$= 70.5, \text{ i.e., } 71$$

Percentile Rank = 71

This answer indicates that 70.5 per cent of the cases fall below the score 63. Usually percentile would make the percentile rank 71 in this problem.

Note: This formula can also be used for finding percentile ranks from simple frequency distributions by assigning $i = L$.

(*i*) Find the percentile rank of the score 71. Use the grouped frequency distribution given in Exercise.

There is a tendency for data to be clustered around or scattered away from the point of central tendency. This tendency is known as dispersion or variability. Measures of dispersion help us in studying the extent to which observations are scattered about the average or the central value.

There are five commonly used measures of dispersion range, quartile deviation, mean deviation, standard deviation and variance. These have been discussed in detail in the present Chapter. However, in computation of further statistics from the measure of dispersion, we always prefer to compute standard deviation to all other measures of dispersion. The computation of percentile and percentile ranks has also been discrussed in this Chapter. It helps in indicating the clear cut relative position of an individual with respect to same attribute in his own group.

Exercises

1. The range is calculated by the formula:

$$R = X_L - X_8$$
$$= 46 - 17 = 29$$
$$R = 29$$

2. (*i*) (*a*)
(*ii*).

Scores	*f*	*"Less than" Cumulative frequency*
90—99	2	75
80—89	12	73
70—79	22	61
60—69	20	39
50—59	14	19
40—49	4	5
30—39	1	1
	N = 75	

(*ii*) (*a*) *Calculation of Q*: Since $N/4 = 75/4 = 18.75$th case lies in the class interval 50 – 59, the quartile class for Q_1 is 50 – 59.

Hence, $1 - 49.5$, $Cf = 5, f = 14, i = 10$.

Putting these values in the formula:

$$Q_1 = L + \frac{\frac{N}{4} - Cf}{f} \times i$$

$$= 49.5 + \frac{18.75 - 5}{14} \times 10$$

$$= 49.5 + \frac{13.75}{14} \times 10$$

$$= 49.5 + 9.82 = 59.32$$

$$Q_1 = 59.32$$

Calculation of Q_3: Since 3N/4 = 3 × 75/4 = 56.25th case falls in the class interval 70 – 79, the quartile class Q_3 is 70 – 79.

Hence, $L = 69.5$, $Cf = 39$, $f = 22$, $i = 10$.

Putting these values in the formula:

$$Q_3 = L + \frac{\frac{3N}{4} - Cf}{f} \times i$$

$$= 69.5 + \frac{\frac{3 \times 75}{4} - 39}{22} \times 10$$

$$= 69.5 + \frac{17.55}{22} \times 10$$

$$= 69.5 + 7.84 = 77.34$$

$$Q_3 = 77.34$$

(ii) (b) $QD = \frac{Q_3 - Q_1}{2}$

As calculated in *ii (a)*, $Q_1 = 159.32$

$Q_3 = 77.34$

$$\text{Hence, } QD = \frac{77.34 - 59.32}{2}$$

$$= \frac{18.02}{2}$$

$$= 9.01$$

$$QD = 9.01$$

(iii)

Scores Classes	*f*	*x*	*fx*	$(X - \bar{x})$ $(x - 67.45)$	$f(X - \bar{x})$
60—62	5	61	305	6.45	32.25
63—65	18	64	1152	3.45	62.1
66—68	42	67	2814	0.45	18.9
69—71	27	70	1890	2.55	63.85
72—74	8	73	584	5.55	44.4
	N = 100	$\Sigma fx = 6745$		$\Sigma f(X - \bar{x}) = 226.5$	

$$\text{Here, Mean} = \frac{\sum fx}{N}$$

$$\bar{x} = \frac{6745}{100} = 67.45$$

$$\text{MD} = \frac{f(x - \bar{x})}{N}$$

$$= \frac{226.5}{100} = 22.65$$

$$\text{MD} = 22.65$$

4. *(i)* *c.*
(ii) *d.*
(iii) *b.*
(iv) *(a)*

S. No.	X	$(X - \bar{x})$ $(X - 60)$	$(X - \bar{x})^2$
1	52	–8	64
2	50	–10	100
3	56	–4	16
4	68	8	64
5	65	5	25
6	62	2	4
7	57	–3	9
8	70	10	100
	$\Sigma X = 480$	$\Sigma(X - \bar{x}) = 382$	

$$\text{Mean} = \frac{\sum X}{N}$$

$$= \frac{480}{8} = 60$$

$$\text{Mean} = 60$$

$$\text{Variance} = \frac{\sum (X-\overline{x})^2}{N}$$

$$= \frac{382}{8} = 47.75$$

$$\text{Variance} = 47.75$$

$$\text{SD} = \sqrt{\frac{\sum (X-\overline{x})^2}{N}}$$

$$= \sqrt{\frac{382}{8}}$$

$$= \sqrt{47.75} = 6.91$$

$$\text{SD} = 6.91$$

(iv) (b)

S. No.	*X*	*X*^{2}
1	52	2704
2	50	2500
3	56	3136
4	68	4624
5	65	4225
6	62	3844
7	57	3249
8	70	4900
	$\Sigma X = 480$	$\Sigma X^2 = 29{,}182$

$$\text{Mean} = \frac{\sum X}{N}$$

$$= \frac{480}{8} = 60$$

$$\text{Mean} = 60$$

$$\text{Variance} = \frac{\sum X^2}{N} - \overline{x}^2$$

$$= \frac{29182}{8} - (60)^2$$

$$= 3647.75 - 3600$$

$$\text{Variance} = 47.75$$

$$SD = \sqrt{\frac{\sum X^2}{N} - \bar{x}^2}$$

$$= \sqrt{\frac{29182}{8} - (60)^2}$$

$$= \sqrt{3647.75 - 3600}$$

$$= \sqrt{47.75} = 6.91$$

$$SD = 6.91$$

(*iv*) (*c*)

S. No.	*x*	*a* = 62 *d* = *x*–62	d^3
1	52	–10	100
2	50	–12	144
3	56	–6	36
4	68	6	36
5	65	3	9
6	62	0	0
7	57	–5	25
8	70	8	64
		$\Sigma d = 16$	$\Sigma d^2 = 414$

$$\text{Variance} = \frac{\sum d^2}{N} - \left\{\frac{\sum d}{N}\right\}^2$$

$$= \frac{414}{8} - \left\{\frac{16}{8}\right\}^2$$

$$= 51.75 - 4 = 47.75$$

$$\text{Variance} = 47.75$$

$$SD = \sqrt{\frac{\sum d^2}{N} - \left\{\frac{\sum d}{N}\right\}^2}$$

$$= \sqrt{\frac{414}{8} - \left\{\frac{16}{8}\right\}^2}$$

$$= \sqrt{51.75 - 4}$$

$$= \sqrt{47.75} = 6.91$$

$$\text{SD} = 6.91$$

(*v*) (*a*)

Class Interval	*f*	*x*	*fx*	$(x-\bar{X})$	$(x-\bar{X})^2$	$f(x-\bar{X})^2$
60—69	1	65	65	27.75	770.062	770.062
50—59	4	55	220	17.75	315.062	1260.25
40—49	10	45	450	7.75	60.062	600.62
30—39	15	35	525	–2.25	5.062	75.937
20—29	8	25	200	– 12.25	150.062	1200.5
10—19	2	15	30	–22.25	495.062	990.125
	N = 40		1490			$\Sigma f(X-\bar{X})^2 = 4897.5$

$$\text{Mean} = \frac{\sum fx}{N}$$

$$= \frac{1490}{40} = 37.25$$

$$\text{Mean} = 37.25$$

$$\text{Variance} = \frac{\sum f(X-\bar{x})^2}{N}$$

$$= \frac{4897.5}{40} = 122.437$$

$$\text{Variance} = 122.437$$

$$\text{SD} = \sqrt{\frac{\sum f(X-\bar{X})^2}{N}}$$

$$= \sqrt{\frac{4897.5}{40}}$$

$$= \sqrt{122.437} = 11.065$$

$$SD = 11.065$$

(*v*) (*b*)

Class Interval	*f*	*x*	*fx*	*fx*^{2}
60—69	1	65	65	5,225
50—59	4	55	220	12,100
40—49	10	45	450	20,250
30—39	15	35	525	18,375
20—29	8	25	200	5,000
10—19	2	15	30	450
	N = 40		$\Sigma fx = 1490$	$\Sigma fx^2 = 60{,}400$

$$\text{Mean} = \frac{\sum fx}{N}$$

$$= \frac{1490}{40} = 37.25$$

$$\text{Mean} = 37.25$$

$$\text{Variance} = \frac{\sum fx^2}{N} - \bar{X}^2$$

$$= \frac{60400}{40} - (37.25)^2$$

$$= 1510 - 1387.56 = 122.437$$

$$\text{Variance} = 122.437$$

$$SD = \sqrt{\frac{\sum fx^2}{N} - \bar{X}^2}$$

$$= \sqrt{\frac{60.400}{40} - (37.25)^2}$$

$$= \sqrt{1510 - 1387.56}$$

$$= \sqrt{122.437} = 11.065$$

$$\text{SD} = 11.065$$

(*v*) (*c*)

Class Interval	*f*	*x*	$d = \frac{x-45}{10}$	*fd*	fd^2
60—69	1	65	2	2	4
50—59	4	55	1	4	16
40—49	10	45	0	0	0
30—39	15	35	–1	–15	15
20—29	8	25	–2	16	32
10—19	2	15	–3	–6	18
	N = 40			$\Sigma fd = 31$	$\Sigma fd^2 = 73$

Here we have taken assumed mean 45

$$\text{Variance} = i^2\left[\frac{\sum fd^2}{N} - \left(\frac{\sum fd}{N}\right)\right]$$

$$= (10)^2\left[\frac{73}{40} - \left(\frac{-31}{40}\right)^2\right]$$

$$= 100 \times [1.825 - .775]$$

$$= 100 \times 1.2244 = 122.44$$

$$\text{Variance} = 122.44$$

$$\text{SD} = i\sqrt{\left[\frac{\sum fd^2}{N} - \left(\frac{\sum fd}{N}\right)^2\right]}$$

$$= 10\sqrt{\frac{73}{40} - \left(\frac{-31}{40}\right)}$$

$$= 10\sqrt{1.825 = .775}$$

$$= 10\sqrt{1.2244}$$

$$= 10 \times 1.11065$$

$$= 11.065$$

$$SD = 11.065$$

5. (*i*) $N_1 = 150$ $\qquad \bar{X}_1 = 120$

$N_2 = 75$ $\qquad \bar{X}_2 = 126$

$$\bar{X}_{12} = \frac{N_1\bar{X}_1 + N_2\bar{X}_2}{N_1 + N_2}$$

$$= \frac{150 \times 120 + 75 \times 126}{150 + 75}$$

$$= \frac{18000 + 9450}{225}$$

$$= \frac{27450}{225} = 122.0$$

$$\bar{X}_{12} = 122$$

$N_1 = 150 \qquad \sigma_1 = 20 \qquad D_1 = (\bar{X}_{12} - \bar{X}_1) = 122 - 120 = 2$

$N_2 = 75 \qquad \sigma_2 = 22 \qquad D_2 = (\bar{X}_{12} - \bar{X}_2) - 122 - 126 = -4$

$$\sigma_{12} = \sqrt{\frac{N_1(\sigma_1^2 + D_1^2) + N_2(\sigma_2^2 + D_2^2)}{N_1 + N_2}}$$

$$= \sqrt{\frac{150[(20)^2 + (2)^2] + 75[(22)^2 + (-4)^2]}{150 + 75}}$$

$$= \sqrt{\frac{150[404 + 4] + 75[484 + 16]}{225}}$$

$$= \sqrt{\frac{150 \times 404 + 75 \times 500}{225}}$$

$$= \sqrt{\frac{60600 + 37500}{225}}$$

$$= \sqrt{436} = 20.88$$

$$\sigma_{12} = 20.88$$

6. (*i*) From the data given in Exercise X we get SD = 11.065 and $\bar{X} = 37.25$. The formula for calculating coefficient of variation is:

$$\text{C.V.} = \frac{\sigma}{\bar{X}} \times 100$$

$$= \frac{11.065}{37.25} \times 100$$

$$= 0.297 \times 100 = 29.7$$

$$\text{C.V.} = 29.7$$

7. (*i*)

Scores	*f*	*"Less than" Cumulative Frequency*
90—99	2	75
80—89	12	73
70—79	22	61
60—69	20	39
50—59	14	19
40—49	4	5
30—39	1	1
	N = 75	

Since $\frac{85N}{100} = \frac{85 \times 75}{100}$ = 63.75th cases lie in 80 – 89, hence P_{85} class is 80 – 89.

Here $L = 79.5$, $Cf = 61$, $f = 12$, $i = 0$.

Putting these values in the formula.

$$P_{85} = L + \frac{\frac{85N}{100} - Cf}{f} \times i$$

$$= 79.5 + \frac{\frac{85 \times 75}{100} - 61}{12} \times 10$$

$$= 79.5 + \frac{63.75 - 61}{12} \times 10$$

$$= 79.5 + \frac{2.75}{12} \times 10$$

$$= 79.5 + 2.29 = 81.79$$

$$P_{85} = 81.79$$

8. (*i*) Percentile Rank of the Score 71, raw-score = 71

$$L = 69.5$$
$$i = 10$$
$$f = 22$$
$$Cf = 39$$
$$N = 75$$

Putting these values in the formula:

$$P_R = \frac{100}{N}\left(\frac{\text{raw score} - L}{i} f + C \times f\right)$$

$$= \frac{100}{75}\left(\frac{71 - 69.5}{10} \times 22 + 39\right)$$

$$= \frac{4}{3}\left(\frac{1.5}{10} \times 22 + 39\right)$$

$$= \frac{4}{3}(3.3 + 39)$$

$$= \frac{4}{3} \times 42.3$$

$$= \frac{169.2}{3} = 56.4, \text{ i.e., } 56$$

Percentile Rank = 56

3

Correlation

We have considered the description of single variable. In education, many situations arise that involve two or more variables. Suppose we have the height and weight of each one of a group of 12 years old girls. We can compute the mean and standard deviation of height and we can do the same for weight. But a very important question may be: Is there any relationship between height and weight? The present Chapter deals with the study of bivariate distribution in which two variables may be interdependent. In case the change in one variable appears to be accompanied by a change in the other variable, the two variables are said to be correlated and this inter-dependence is called Correlation.

In some cases, we find that the two variables seem to be unrelated, i.e., uncorrelated. It means that they are having zero correlation. In other instances, the variables tend to rise and fall together, that is an increase in one is generally accompanied by an increase in the other and a decrease in one is accompanied by a decrease in the other. This relationship is referred to as a positive correlation. For example, we accept a positive correlation between height and weight of a group of students. Another kind of correlation is negative correlation. This occurs when an increase in one variable is accompanied by a decrease in the other or a decrease in the first is accompanied by an increase in the second. Thus there is a negative relationship between the two variables. For example, there may be a negative correlation between the scores on intelligence test and the length of time required to solve a set of problems.

METHODS OF STUDYING CORRELATION

The following are the main methods to study the correlation between the two variables.

- Scatter diagram method.
- Pearson's coefficient of correlation.
- Spearman's coefficient of rank correlation.

Scatter Diagram Method

Scatter diagram is a graphic device for drawing certain conclusions about the correlation between the two variables. The Scatter diagram will enable us to determine whether the relationship is positive or negative. In constructing a Scatter diagram, we draw a horizontal axis along which we will locate one variable (say x) and a vertical axis along which we will locate the other variable (say y). A point will be positioned on the Scatter diagram by going along the horizontal axis until we find the value of score x and from that point we will proceed vertically until we reach the height for the corresponding value of y. The placement of these points on the graph reveals the change in the variable as to whether they change in the same or in the opposite directions.

In case all the dots are lying on a straight line of positive slope as in Fig. 3.1, we have a perfect positive correlation between the two variables, i.e., $r = +1$. Similarly, if all the dots are lying on a straight line of negative slope as in Fig. 3.2, correlation between two variables will be perfectly negative, i.e., $r = -1$. If the dots do not follow a pattern along with a straight line as in Fig. 3.3, we have no correlation or zero correlation. If the dots be close to a straight line of positive slope (Fig. 3.4) or negative slope (Fig. 3.5), we have a high degree of positive or negative correlation between the two variables.

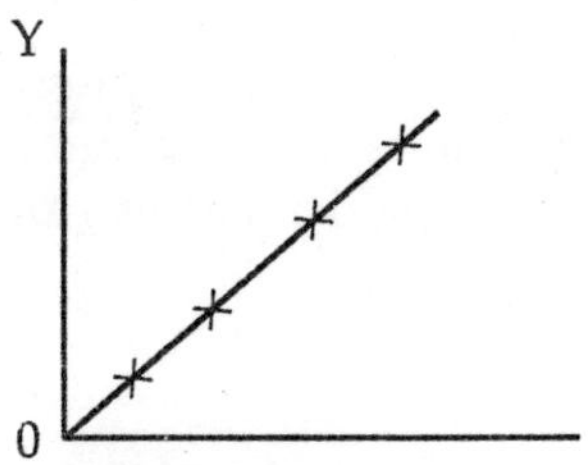

Perfect Positive Correlation $r = +1$

Fig. 3.1

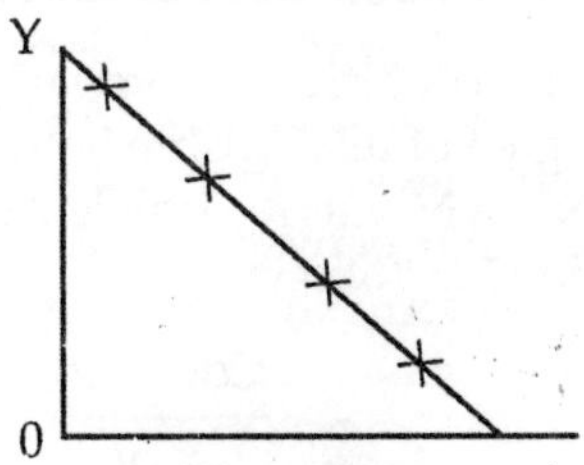

Perfect Negative Correlation $r = -1$

Fig. 3.2

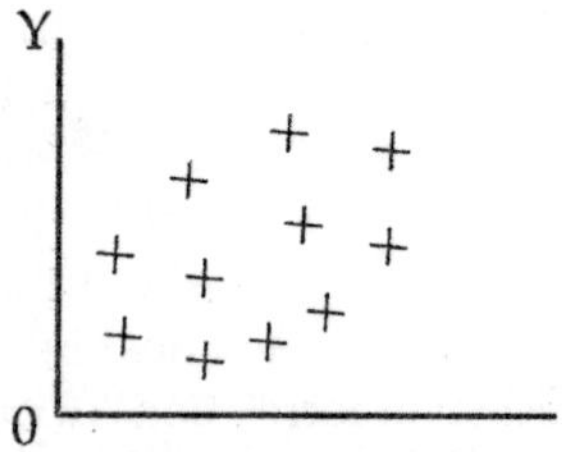

Zero Correlation
$r = 0$

Fig. 3.3

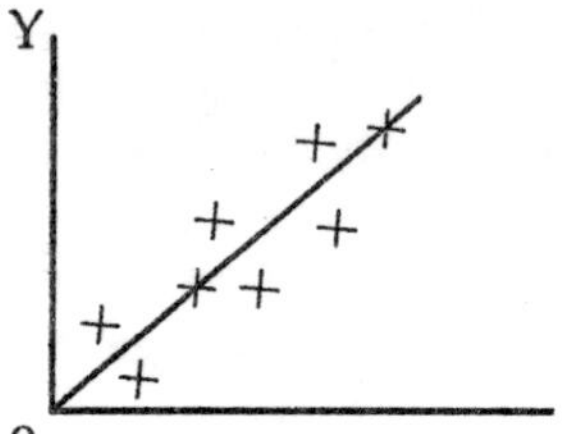

High Degree Positive Correlation

Fig. 3.4

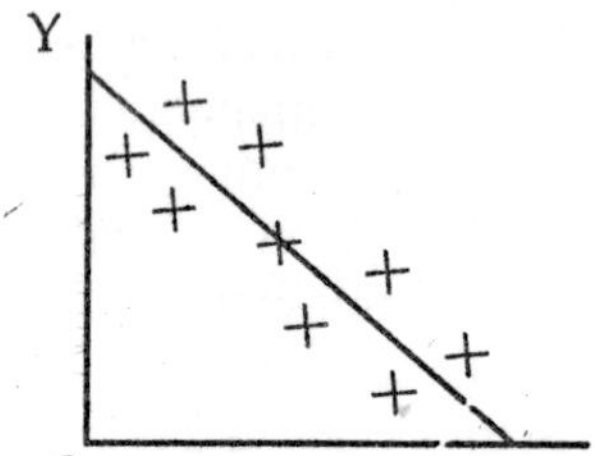

High Degree Negative Correlation

Fig. 3.5

Scatter Diagrams Showing Various Degrees of Correlation

From the above degrees of correlation, it is clear that the correlation between two variables, varying from –1 to +1, is a measure of their relationship. The greater the scatter of the dots from the straight line on the graph, the lesser the correlation.

Pearson's Coefficient of Correlation

Pearson's coefficient of correlation is a pure number which expresses the degree of relationship between two variables. It is also known as Product Moment coefficient of correlation. It is denoted by r and is defined as follows:

$$r = \frac{\text{Cov}(x, y)}{x \quad y}$$

Where, Cov (x, y) = Covariance between x and y

x = S.D. of x series

y = S.D. of y series.

The value of coefficient of correlation r shall always lie between –1 and +1, the correlation between two variables is said to be perfectly negative or perfectly positive. An intermediate value of r between –1 and +1 indicates the extent of linear relationship between x and y whereas its sign tells about the direction of this relationship. The value $r = 0$ means no linear relationship between the two variables. A coefficient of correlation is a pure number which is independent of the unit of measurement.

Computation of Pearson's Coefficient of Correlation for Ungrouped Data

The Pearson's coefficient of correlation, r, can be computed by using one of the following methods:

- Direct Method.
- Short-cut Method.

Direct Method

In case of ungrouped data, the formula for computing coefficient of correlation, r, is as follows:

$$r = \frac{\sum (X - \bar{x})(y - \bar{y})}{\sqrt{\sum (X - \bar{x})^2 \sum (y - \bar{y})^2}}$$

where,

$\sum (X - \bar{x})(y - \bar{y})$ = the sum of the products of deviations of x and y from $\bar{x}$ and $\bar{y}$ respectively.

$\sum (X - \bar{x})^2$ = the sum of squared deviations of x taken from mean $\bar{x}$.

$\sum (X \quad \bar{y})^2$ = the sum of squared deviations of y taken from mean $\bar{y}$.

The procedure for determining the r involves the following steps:

- Find the means $\bar{x}, \bar{y}$ from x and y Scores.
- Subtract $\bar{x}$ from each x and $\bar{y}$ from each y to get $(X - \bar{x})$ and $(y - \bar{y})$.

- Take square of $(X'-\bar{x})$ and $(y-\bar{y})$ to get $(X-\bar{x})^2 (y-\bar{y})^2$.
- Multiply each pair of $X-\bar{x}$ and $y-\bar{y}$ values to get the $(X-\bar{x})(y-\bar{y})$.
- Sum all $(X-\bar{x})^2, (y-\bar{y})^2$ to get $\sum(X-\bar{x})^2 \sum(y-\bar{y})^2$.
- Sum all $(X-\bar{x})(y-\bar{y})$ to get $\sum(X-\bar{x})(y-\bar{y})$.
- Substitute these values into the formula and compute *r*.

The computation procedure will be clear from the following examples:

Example 1:

Calculate Pearson's Coefficient of Correlation from the following scores of a group of students in two subjects:

Students :	1	2	3	4	5	6	7	8	9	10
Marks in Sanskrit (x) :	13	16	11	17	16	12	19	20	20	16
Marks in English (y) :	14	19	10	16	15	18	26	29	23	10

Solution:

Students	x	y	$x-\bar{x}$	$y-\bar{y}$	$(x-x)^2$	$(y-\bar{y})^2$	$x-\bar{x}(y-\bar{y})$
1	13	14	–3	–4	9	16	12
2	16	19	0	1	0	1	0
3	11	10	–5	–8	25	64	40
4	17	16	1	–2	1	4	–2
5	16	15	0	–3	0	9	0
6	12	18	–4	0	16	0	0
7	19	26	3	8	9	64	24
8	20	29	4	11	16	121	44
9	20	23	4	5	16	25	20
10	16	10	0	–8	0	64	0
N = 10	$\Sigma x = 160$	$\Sigma y = 180$			$\Sigma(x-\bar{x})^{-2} = 92$	$\Sigma(y-\bar{y})^{-2} = 363$	$\Sigma(x-x)-(y-\bar{y}) = 138$

$$\text{Here, } x = \frac{\sum x}{N} = \frac{160}{10} = 16$$

$$y = \frac{\sum y}{N} = \frac{180}{10} = 18$$

$$r = \frac{\sum(x-\bar{x})(y-\bar{y})}{\sqrt{\sum(x-\bar{x})^2 \sum(y-\bar{y})^2}}$$

Putting the values from the above table, we have:

$$r = \frac{138}{\sqrt{92 \times 368}}$$

$$r = \frac{138}{\sqrt{33856}} = \frac{138}{184} = 0.75$$

$$r = 0.75$$

Another formula using raw scores, which is equivalent to that previously stated used for finding r is.

$$r = \frac{N\sum Xy - \sum X \sum y}{\sqrt{\left[N\sum X^2 - \left(\sum X\right)^2\right]\left[N\sum y^2 - (\Sigma y)^2\right]}}$$

where,

N = the number of paired observations.
Σxy = the sum of the products of the scores for x and y.
Σx = the sum of scores of x.
Σy = the sum of scores of y.
Σx^2 = the sum of squared scores of x.
Σy^2 = the sum of squared scores of y.

This formula is simpler than the previous one, since here raw scores are used rather than deviations. This method can be described by the following steps:

- Square each raw score of x and y to obtain x^2 and y^2.
- Multiply each x with corresponding y to obtain xy.
- Sum all x and y to obtain Σx and Σy.
- Apply the formula to calculate r.

Steps involved in calculating '*r*' by using the 'raw score' formula will be clear from the following example.

Example 2:

Compute the coefficient of correlation '*r*' for the scores of *x* and *y* given in Example 1.

Students	x	y	x^2	y^2	xy
1	13	14	169	196	182
2	16	19	256	361	304
3	11	10	121	100	110
4	17	16	289	256	272
5	16	15	256	225	240
6	12	18	144	324	216
7	19	26	361	676	494
8	20	29	400	841	580
9	20	23	400	529	460
10	16	10	256	100	160
N = 10	$\Sigma x = 160$	$\Sigma y = 180$	$\Sigma x^2 = 2652$	$\Sigma y^2 = 3608$	$\Sigma xy = 3018$

Putting these values in the formula to compute *r*:

$$r = \frac{N\Sigma xy - \Sigma x\Sigma y}{\sqrt{\left[N\Sigma x^2 - (\Sigma x)^2\right]\left[N\Sigma y^2 - (\Sigma y)^2\right]}}$$

$$= \frac{(10 \times 3018) - (160 \times 180)}{\sqrt{\left[10 \times 2652 - (160)^2\right]\left[10 \times 3608 - (180)^2\right]}}$$

$$= \frac{30180 - 28800}{\sqrt{[26520 - 25600][36080 - 32400]}}$$

$$= \frac{1380}{\sqrt{920 \times 3680}}$$

$$= \frac{1380}{\sqrt{3385600}}$$

$$= \frac{1380}{1840} = 0.75$$

$$r = 0.75$$

Short-cut Method

According to this method, the coefficient of correlation 'r' is calculated by using the following formula:

$$r = \frac{N\Sigma dxdy - \Sigma dx - \Sigma dy}{\sqrt{\left[N\Sigma dx^2 - (\Sigma dx)^2\right]\left[N\Sigma dy^2 - (\Sigma dy)^2\right]}}$$

where,

N = the number of paired observations.
$dx = x - a$ deviation of x taken from assumed mean a.
$dy = y - b$ deviation of y taken from assumed mean b.
Σdx^2 = the sum of squared deviations dx^2.
Σdy^2 = the sum of squared deviations dy^2.
$\Sigma dxdy$ = the sum of products of deviations dx and dy.

The steps involved in the computation procedure by this method may be listed as:

- Find assumed means a and b of x-series and y-series in the middle of x-series and y-series.
- Subtract a from each x score to obtain $dx = x - a$. Similarly subtract b from each y-score to obtain $dy = y - b$.
- Multiply each dx with the corresponding dy to obtain $dxdy$.
- Square each dx and dy to obtain dx^2 and dy^2.
- Sum all dx and dy to get Σdx and Σdy.
- Sum all dx^2, dy^2 and $dxdy$ to obtain Σdx^2, Σdy^2 and $\Sigma dxdy$.
- Apply the formula to compute 'r'. The following example will clear all the steps of computation procedure.

Example 3:

Calculate coefficient of correlation 'r' for the data given in Example 1 by short-cut method.

Solution:

Students	*x*	*y*	*dx*	*dy*	*dx*²	*dy*²	*dxdy*
1	13	14	–2	6	4	36	12
2	16	19	1	–1	1	1	–1
3	11	10	–4	–10	16	100	40
4	17	16	2	–4	4	16	–8
5	16	15	1	–5	1	25	–5
6	12	18	–3	–2	9	4	6
7	19	26	4	6	16	36	24
8	20	29	5	9	25	81	45
9	20	23	5	3	25	9	15
10	16	10	1	10	1	100	–10
N=10			$\Sigma dx=10$	$\Sigma dy=-20$	$\Sigma dx^2=102$	$\Sigma dy^2=408$	$\Sigma dxdy=118$

Since x-series varies from 11 to 20, the assumed mean '*a*' can be taken as 15. Similarly, for y-series we take assumed mean '*b*' as 20.

Putting the values in the formula.

$$r = \frac{N\Sigma dxdy - \Sigma dx - \Sigma dy}{\sqrt{\left[N\Sigma dx^2 - (\Sigma dx)^2\right]\left[N\Sigma dy^2 - (\Sigma dy)^2\right]}}$$

$$= \frac{(10\times 118) - 10\times(-20)}{\sqrt{\left[10\,(102)-(10)^2\right]\left[10(408)-(-20)^2\right]}}$$

$$= \frac{1180+200}{\sqrt{[1020-100][4080-400]}}$$

$$= \frac{1380}{\sqrt{920\times 3680}}$$

$$= \frac{1380}{\sqrt{3385600}}$$

$$= \frac{1380}{1840} = 0.75$$

$$r = 0.75$$

Computation of Pearson's Coefficient of Correlation for Grouped Data

In case the number of pairs of measurements on two variables x and y are large, we group the measurements in the form of a two-way frequency distribution which is also called a bivariate frequency distribution. To clarify the idea, we consider a bivariate data concerned with the scores earned by a class of 25 students in Science and Arithmetic.

Marks in Science (y)	*Marks in Arithmetic (x)*				
	30—39	40—49	50—59	60—69	Total
30—39	3	1	1	—	5
40—49	2	6	1	2	11
50—59	1	2	2	1	6
60—69	—	1	1	1	3
Total	6	10	5	4	25

In this table, we observe that the frequency in the first cell is 3. It means that there are three students whose scores in Science as well as in Arithmetic fall in scores class 30—39. Similarly, the frequency in the second cell is 2. It means that there are 2 students whose scores in Science fall in class 40—49 while their scores in Arithmetic fall in class 30—39. Other cell frequencies may also be similarly interpreted. Marginal column and row totals in the above table show the distribution of frequencies in respect of variables x and y respectively.

The formula for computing Pearson's coefficient of correlation in a bivariate frequency distribution is as follows:

$$r = \frac{N\Sigma fdxdy - \Sigma fdx - \Sigma fdy}{\sqrt{\left[N\Sigma fdx^2 - (\Sigma fdx)^2\right]\left[N\Sigma fdy^2 - (\Sigma fdy)^2\right]}}$$

This formula is similar to that used for ungrouped data. The only difference is that the deviations in the formula are also multiplied by the respective frequencies. The formula involves the following steps in computation.

- Find mid-points of the classes as x and y for both the variables.
- Consider deviations for both the variables and denote them as dx and dy respectively.
- Multiply dx, dy and the corresponding frequency in the cell and write the resulting figure in the upper right hand corner of the cell.
- Add all these values in the cells to get $\Sigma fdxdy$.
  - — Multiply dx by the frequencies of the variables x and obtain the sum Σfdx.

— Multiply *dy* by the respective frequencies of the variable *y* and add them to get *fdy*.
— Multiply dx^2 by the corresponding frequencies of the variable *x* and obtain the sum Σfdx^2.
— Multiply dy^2 by the corresponding frequencies of the variable *y* and obtain the sum Σfdy^2.
— Substitute these values in the formula to compute '*r*'.
The computation procedure is clarified in the following example:

Example 4:

Calculate the coefficient of correlation between marks obtained by 25 students in Science and Arithmetic given in the above table.

			Marks in Arithmetic (x)							
			30–39	40–49	50–59	60–69				
		x	34.5	44.5	54.5	64.5				
Marks in Science (y)	*y*	*dx* / *dy*	–1	0	1	2	*f*	*fdy*	fdy^2	*fdx.dy*
30–39	34.5	–2	3 [6]	1 [0]	1 [–2]	0 [0]	5	–10	20	4
40–49	44.5	–1	2 [2]	6 [0]	1 [–2]	2 [–4]	11	–11	11	–3
50–59	54.5	0	1 [0]	2 [0]	2 [0]	1 [2]	6	0	0	0
60–69	64.5	1	0 [0]	1 [0]	1 [3]	1 [2]	3	3	3	3
		f	6	10	5	4	25	–18	34	4
		fdx	–6	0	5	8				
		fdx^2	6	0	5	16				
		fdxdy	8	0	–2	–2				

Here, $\Sigma fdx = 7$ $\Sigma fdx^2 = 27$ $\Sigma fdxdy = 4$
$\Sigma fdy = -18$ $\Sigma fdy^2 = 34$ $N = 25$

Substituting these values in the formula for computing *r*.

$$r = \frac{N\sum fdxdy - \left(\sum fdx\right)\left(\sum fdy\right)}{\sqrt{\left[N\sum fdx^2 - \left(\sum fdx\right)^2\right]\left[N\sum fdy^2 - \left(\sum fdy\right)^2\right]}}$$

$$r = \frac{25 \times 4 - (7) \quad (-18)}{\sqrt{[25 \times 27 - (7)^2][25 \times 34 - (-18)^2]}}$$

$$= \frac{100 + 126}{2\sqrt{[675 - 49][850 - 324]}}$$

$$= \frac{226}{2\sqrt{626 \times 526}}$$

$$= \frac{226}{2\sqrt{329276}}$$

$$= \frac{226}{573.83} = 0.39$$

$$r = 8.39$$

Exercises

1. Which one of the following correlation coefficients shows the greatest amount of relationship between variables?
   (*a*) .65
   (*b*) .52
   (*c*) –.95
   (*d*) .00
2. Find the correlation between the following two sets of scores using (*a*) Direct Method, (*b*) Raw score formula and (*c*) Short-cut Method.

Individual:	1	2	3	4	5	6	7	8	9	10
Text X :	13	12	10	8	7	6	6	4	3	1
Text Y :	7	11	3	7	2	12	6	2	9	6

Spearman's Coefficient of Rank Correlation

Pearson's coefficient of correlation measures the relationship between two quantitative variables. But in many situations, it is not always possible to make definite measurements on the variables. For example, the evaluation of a group of students on the basis of leadership ability, the ordering of women in a healthy contest etc.

Example 6:

Find rank coefficient of correlation for the following data:

S. No.	*1*	*2*	*3*	*4*	*5*	*6*	*7*	*8*
X	81	78	73	73	69	68	62	52
Y	10	12	18	18	18	22	20	24

Solution:

S. No.	X	Y	*Rx*	*Ry*	*(Rx–Ry)*	d^2
1	81	10	1	8	7	49
2	78	12	2	7	–5	25
3	73	18	3.5	5	–1.5	2.25
4	73	18	3.5	5	–1.5	2.25
5	69	18	5	5	0	0
6	68	22	6	2	4	16
7	62	20	7	3	4	16
8	52	24	8	1	7	49
N = 8						$\Sigma d^2 = 159.80$

In the above example, in x-series, 3rd and 4th students are found to achieve the same score 73. These students would have got 3rd and 4th position in order of merit. Hence, the average of these two ranks 3rd and 4th i.e. 3.5 is given to both these students. Similarly, in y-series, 3rd, 4th and 5th students are given the same rank 5 (the average of 4.5 and 6) because they are having the same score 18.

Putting the value of $\Sigma d^2 = 159.5$ and N = 8 in the formula:

$$r = 1 - \frac{6\sum d^2}{N(N^2-1)}$$

$$= 1 - \frac{6 \times 159.5}{8(64-1)}$$

$$= 1 - \frac{957}{504}$$

$$= 1 - 1.90 = .90$$

$$r = 0.90$$

1. Find the rank correlation coefficient between the following two sets of scores.

Individuals:	*1*	*2*	*3*	*4*	*5*	*6*	*7*	*8*	*9*	*10*	*11*
Text X	80	45	55	56	58	60	65	68	70	75	85
Text Y	82	86	50	48	60	62	64	65	70	74	99

The present chapter has dealt with the study of bivariate distributions in which two variables may be inter-dependent. In case the change in one variable appears to be accompanied by a change in the other variable, the two variables are said to be correlated and this inter-dependence is called correlation. If the relationship between two variables is such that larger values of one tend to associate with larger values of another, the correlation is said to be positive. But if larger value of one variable tend to associate with smaller values of the other, correlation is said to be negative.

The value of coefficient of correlation shall always lie between –1 and +1. When $r = +1$ or –1, the correlation between two variables is said to be perfectly positive or perfectly negative. There are three methods of studying correlation—Scatter diagram method, Spearman's coefficient of correlation and Pearson's coefficient of correlation. These have been discussed in detail in the present chapter.

Exercises

1. (*i*) *d*
   (*ii*) *c*
   (*iii*) (*a*) By Direct Method

Individuals	x	y	$X-\bar{x}$ $(X-7)$	$y-\bar{y}$ $(y-6.5)$	$(x-\bar{x})^2$	$(y-\bar{y})^2$	$(X-\bar{x})(y-\bar{y})$
1	13	7	6	0.5	36	0.25	3.0
2	12	11	5	4.5	25	20.25	22.5
3	10	3	3	–3.5	9	12.25	10.5
4	8	7	1	0.5	1	6.25	0.5
5	7	2	0	–4.5	0	20.25	0
6	6	12	–1	5.5	1	30.25	–5.5
7	6	6	–1	–0.5	1	0.25	0.5
8	4	2	–3	4.5	9	20.25	13.5
9	3	9	–4	2.5	16	6.25	-10.0
10	1	6	–6	–0.5	36	0.25	3.0
$N = 10$	$\Sigma x = 70$	$\Sigma y = 65$			$\Sigma(x-\bar{x})^2 = 134$	$\Sigma(y-\bar{y})^2 = 110.50$	17.0

Here, $\bar{X} = \frac{\Sigma x}{N} = \frac{70}{10} = 7$

$$\bar{Y} = \frac{\Sigma y}{N} = \frac{65}{10} = 6.5$$

Therefore,

$$\Sigma(X-\bar{x})(y-\bar{y}) = 17$$

$$\Sigma(x-X)^2 = 134$$

$$\Sigma(y-\bar{y})^2 = 110.50$$

Putting these values in the formula to compute r.

$$r = \frac{\Sigma(X-\bar{x})(y-\bar{y})}{\sqrt{\Sigma(X-\bar{X})^2\,\Sigma(y-\bar{y})^2}}$$

$$r = \frac{17}{110.5 \times 134}$$

$$r = \frac{17}{\sqrt{14807}}$$

$$r = \frac{17}{121.68} = 0.139$$

$$r = 0.139$$

(*iii*) (*b*) By Using Raw Score Formula

Students	x	y	x^2	y^2	xy
1	13	7	169	49	91
2	12	11	144	121	132
3	10	3	100	9	30
4	8	7	64	49	56
5	7	2	49	4	14
6	6	12	36	144	72
7	6	6	36	36	36
8	4	2	16	4	8
9	3	9	9	81	27
10	1	6	1	36	6
N = 10	$\Sigma x = 70$	$\Sigma y = 65$	$\Sigma x^2 = 624$	$\Sigma y^2 = 533$	$\Sigma xy = 472$

Therefore, $\Sigma x = 70$ $\quad \Sigma x^2 = 624$ $\quad \Sigma xy = 472$

$\Sigma y = 65$ $\quad \Sigma y^2 = 533$ $\quad N = 10$

Substituting these values in the formula to calculate r.

$$r = \frac{N\Sigma xy - \Sigma x - \Sigma y}{\sqrt{[N\Sigma x^2 - (\Sigma x)^2][N\Sigma y^2 - (\Sigma y)^2]}}$$

$$= \frac{10\times 472 - 70\times 65}{\sqrt{[10\times 624 - (70)^2][10\times 533 - (65)^2]}}$$

$$= \frac{4720 - 4550}{\sqrt{[6240 - 4900][5330 - 4225]}}$$

$$= \frac{170}{\sqrt{1340\times 1105}}$$

$$= \frac{170}{\sqrt{1480700}}$$

$$= \frac{170}{1216.84} = 0.139$$

$$r = 0.139$$

(*iii*) (*c*) By Using Short-cut Method

Students	*x*	*y*	*dx*	*dy*	dx^2	dy^2	*dxdy*
1	13	7	7	1	49	1	7
2	12	11	6	5	36	25	30
3	10	3	4	–3	16	9	–12
4	8	7	2	1	–4	1	2
5	7	2	1	–4	1	16	–4
6	6	12	0	6	0	36	0
7	6	6	0	0	0	0	0
8	4	2	–2	–4	4	16	8
9	3	9	–3	3	9	9	9
10	1	6	–5	0	25	0	0
N = 10			$\Sigma dx = 10$	$\Sigma dy = 5$	$\Sigma dx^2 = 144$	$\Sigma dy^2 = 113$	$\Sigma dxdy = 22$

In both the series x and y, the assumed mean 'a' and 'b' has been taken as 6 to get dx and dy.

Therefore, $\Sigma dx = 10$ $\Sigma dx^2 = 144$ $\Sigma dxdy = 22$

$\Sigma dy = 5$ $\Sigma dy^2 = 113$ $N = 10$

Putting the values in the formula to compute r.

$$r = \frac{N\Sigma dxdy - \Sigma dx \Sigma dy}{\sqrt{[N\Sigma dx^2 - (dx)^2][N\Sigma dy^2 - \Sigma(dy)^2]}}$$

$$= \frac{10\times 22 - 10\times 5}{\sqrt{[10\times 144 - (10)^2][10\times 113 - (5)^2]}}$$

$$= \frac{220-50}{\sqrt{[1440-100][1130-25]}}$$

$$= \frac{170}{\sqrt{1340\times 1105}}$$

$$= \frac{170}{\sqrt{1480700}} = 0.139$$

$$= \frac{170}{1216.84} = 0.139$$

$$r = 0.139$$

2. (*i*) Rank Correlation Coefficient

S. No.	*X*	*Y*	*Rx*	*Ry*	*(Rx–Ry)*	d^2
1	80	82	2	3	–1	1
2	45	86	11	2	9	81
3	55	50	10	10	0	0
4	56	48	9	11	–2	4
5	58	60	8	9	–1	1
6	60	62	7	8	–1	1
7	65	64	6	7	–1	1
8	68	65	5	6	–1	1
9	70	70	4	5	–1	1
10	75	74	3	4	–1	1
11	85	99	1	1	0	0
N = 11						$\Sigma d^2 = 92$

Putting these values in the formula

$$r = 1 - \frac{6\Sigma d^2}{N(N^2 - 1)}$$

$$= 1 - \frac{6 \times 92}{11(11^2 - 1)}$$

$$= 1 - \frac{552}{11 \times 120}$$

$$= 1 - \frac{552}{1320}$$

$$= 1 - 0.418$$

$$= 0.582$$

$$r = 0.582$$

4

Normal Probability Curve (NPC)

One of the most important continuous distribution is the normal probability distribution. A large number of distribution arising in studies of natural, social and psychological phenomena conform to normal. The graphical expression of the normal distribution, called the normal curve, is the bell shaped smooth symmetrical curve. Often the distribution of quantitative data that we observe show concentration of frequency near a central value and spread over symmetrically on both sides. The tendency of quantitative data for a large number of measurements, give rise to the symmetrical bell shaped form of normal curve.

Example of NPC

Examples of such data would be:

- scores on many educational and psychological tests, assuming a fairly large number of test items and a fairly large number of persons taking the test.
- measurement of some physical variables such as height, weight, etc.
- measurements which depend upon many causes, an example would be a distribution of mental ability for a class in a college.

THE EQUATION OF THE NORMAL CURVE

The equation of the normal curve is

$$f(x) = \frac{1}{\sigma\sqrt{2\pi}} \exp\left\{-\frac{1}{2}\left(\frac{x-\mu}{\sigma}\right)^2\right\}, -\infty < \mathrm{x} < \infty$$

where

X = continuous random variable.

μ = the mean of the distribution, and
σ = the standard deviation of the distribution.

The raw scores can be converted into standard scores by the following transformation:

$$z = \frac{x-\mu}{\sigma}$$

The standard scores have a mean zero and standard deviation one. In case 0 and 1, the normal equation becomes

$$f(z) = \frac{1-½(z^2)}{\sqrt{2\pi}} c - \infty < z < \infty$$

In this case the variable z is called standard normal variate and distribution is called standardised normal distribution.

PROPERTIES OF THE NORMAL CURVE

Some of the important properties of normal curve are given below:

- If we plot the curve for the values of standard normal variate z and the corresponding probabilities, it is of the shape given in Fig. 4.0.

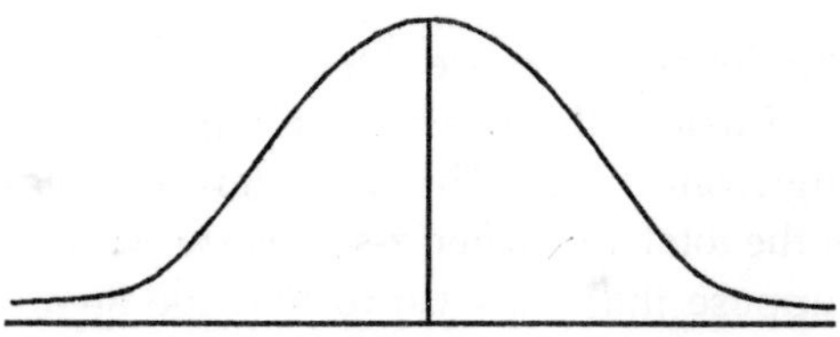

Fig. 4.0

- The curve is perfectly symmetrical about a vertical axis through the mean μ, i.e., if we fold the curve along this vertical axis, the two values of the curve would coincide.
- Because of symmetry, mean, median and mode of the distribution are identical.
- The normal curve approaches the horizontal axis asymptotically, i.e., the curve continues to decrease in height on both ends away from mean but never touches the horizontal axis.
  Theoretically, it extends from— ∝ to + σ.

- The height of the curve decline symmetrically in either direction from the maximum point at. Hence, the heights for values $x = \mu \pm k$, are equal.
- The area under normal curve is unity.
- Since the shape of normal curve is completely determined with its parameters μ and σ, the area under the curve bounded by the two ordinates also depends on these parameters. Some important areas under the curve bounded by ordinates at σ, 2σ and 3σ distances away from mean in either direction are given.
- The area between ordinates at $x = \mu - \sigma$ and $x = \mu + \sigma$ is 0.6827 or 68.27%.
- The area between ordinates at $x = \mu - 2\sigma$ and $x = \mu + 2\sigma$ is 0.9545 or 95.45%.
- The area between ordinates at $x = \mu - 3\sigma$ and $x = \mu + 3\sigma$ is 0.9973 or 99.73%.

Thus practically, the whole area under the normal curve lies between limits $\mu \pm 3\sigma$ which are also called 3σ limits.

AREA UNDER THE NORMAL CURVE

Table of area under normal curve shows the proportion of the area between the ordinate at the mean of standard normal variate and at z extending from 0 to 3. The table can be used to find the proportion of the total area when z-scores are given.

Let us suppose that we wish to find the area between the ordinates at z = 0 and z = 1. We note from this table that this area is 0.3413. Thus approximately 34% of the total area falls between the mean and one standard deviation unit above the mean. For better understanding, consider the following situations:

(*i*) If z_0 is a negative value, then

$$P(z \leq z_0) = 0.5 - A$$

Where A is the area between ordinates at $z = 0$ and $z = z_0$. The required reg on is shaded region by dots.

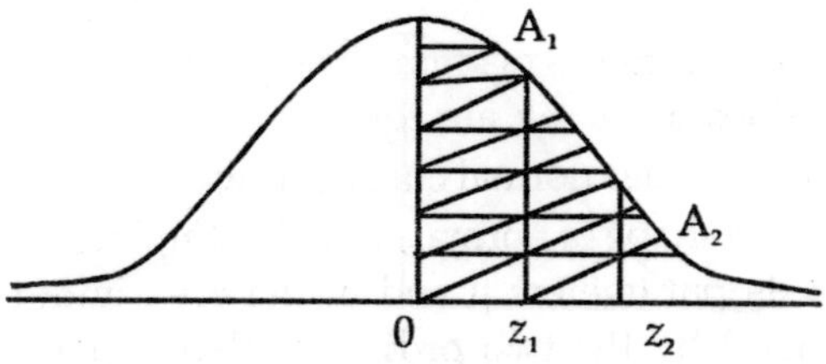

Fig. 4.1

(*ii*) If z_0 is positive number then

$$P(z = z_0) = 0.5 + A$$

Where A is the area between the ordinates at $z - 0$ and $z = z_0$.

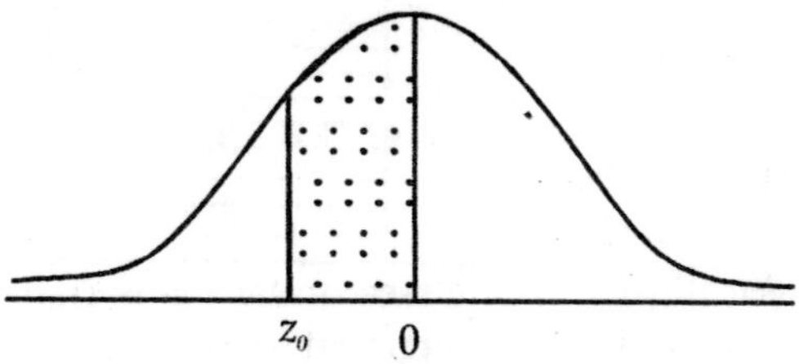

Fig. 4.2

(*iii*) If z_1 is negative and z_2 is a positive number then

$$P(z_1 < z < z_2) = A_1 + A_2$$

Where A_1 is the area between ordinates at $z = 0$ and $z = z_1$ and A_2 is the area between ordinates at $z = 0$ and $z = z_2$.

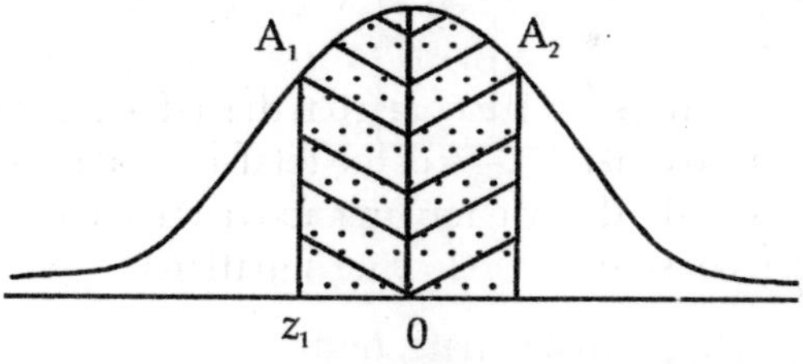

Fig. 4.3

(*iv*) If z_1 and z_2 both are positive numbers then

$$P(z_1 \leq z \leq z_2) = A - A_1$$

Where A_1 is the area between ordinates at $z = 0$ and $z = z_1$, A_2 is the area between ordinates at $z = 0$ and $z = z_2$.

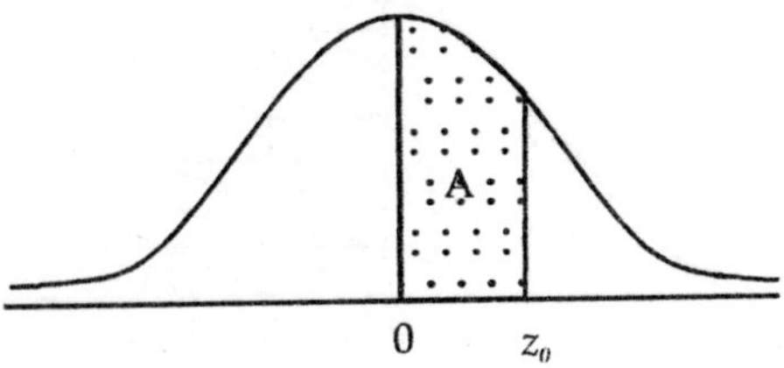

Fig. 4.4

(*v*) If z_0 is a positive number then

$$P(z \geq z_0) = 0.5 - A$$

Where A is the area between the ordinates at $z = 0$ and $z = z_0$.

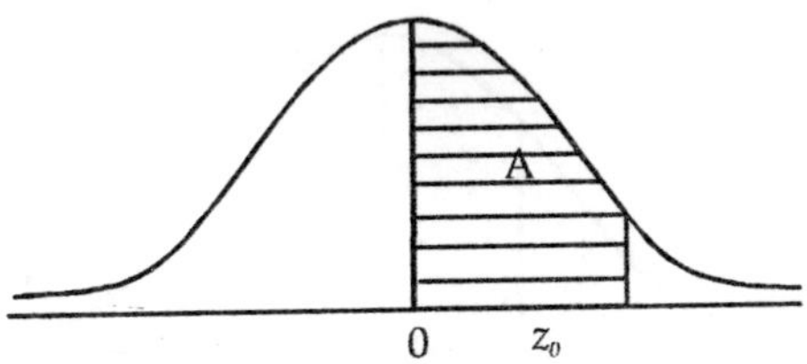

Fig. 4.5

(*vi*) If z_0 is a negative number then

$$P(z \geq z_0) = 0.5 + A$$

Where A is the area between the ordinates at $z = 0$ and $z = z_0$.

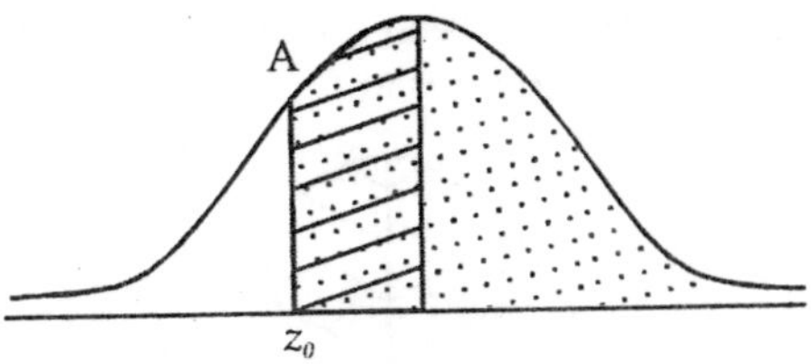

Fig. 4.6

Example 1:

If z is a standard normal variate, find

(*i*) $P(0 < z < 2)$
(*ii*) $P(-1 < z < 0)$
(*iii*) $P(-2 < z < 2)$

Solution:

Since z is a standard normal variable, table under normal curve can be used to determine the probabilities.

(*i*) To find P $(0 < z < 2)$

Here the required area is between the ordinates at $z = 0$ and $z = 2$ from table

$$P(0 < z < 2) = 0.4773$$

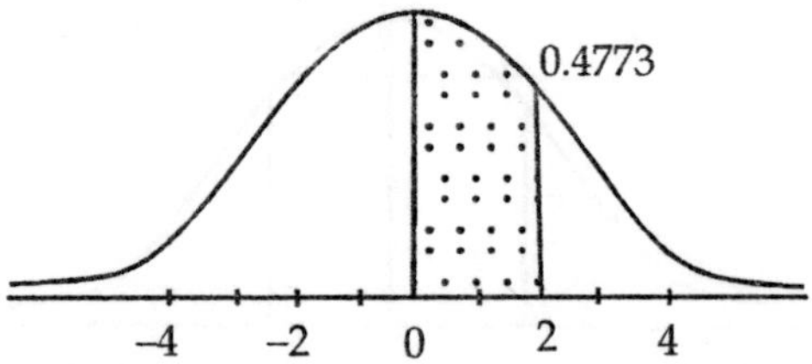

(*ii*) To find P $(-1 < z < 0)$

Since normal curve is symmetrical about the ordinate at $z = 0$, the area between the ordinates at $z = -1$ and $z = 0$ is same as the area between the ordinate at $z = 0$ and $z = 1$.

Hence

$$P(-1 < z < 0) = P(0 < z < 1)$$
$$= 0.3413 \text{ (from table of area under curve).}$$

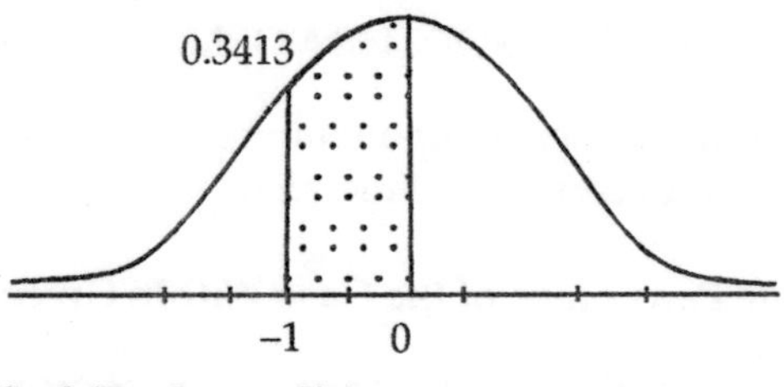

(*iii*) To find (P—2 <z < 2)

$$\begin{aligned} P(-2 < z < 2) &= P(-2 < z < 0) + P(0 < z < 2) \\ &= P(0 < z < 2) + P(0 < z < 2) \\ &= 0.4773 + 0.4773 \\ &= 0.9546 \end{aligned}$$

Example 2:

What percentage of the cases in a normal frequency distribution falls between $z = -1.00$ and $z = 1.50$.

Solution:

We have to find the $P(-1 < z < 1.5)$

This we can find as

$$P(-1 < z < 1.5) = P_1(-1 < z < 0) + P(0 < z < .5)$$

$= P(0 < z < 1.0) + P(0 < z < 1.5)$
= (from symmetric property of normal curve)
$= 0.3413 + 0.4332$
$= 0.7745$

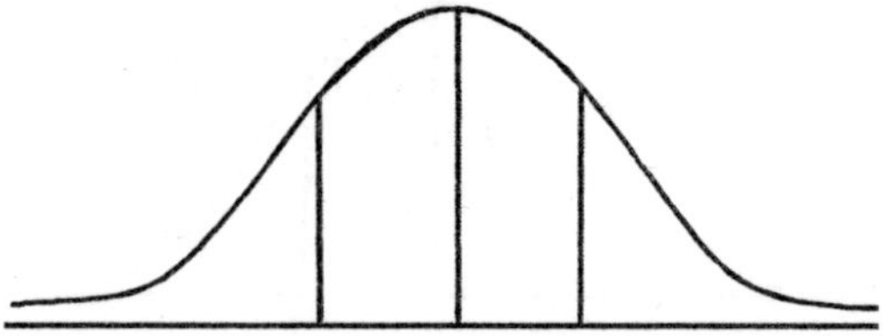

Therefore, 77.45% cases falls between $z = -1.00$ and $z = 1.50$.

Exercises

1. In a normal frequency distribution, what per cent of the scores lies between z-scores of –1.50 and 1.50?
2. In a normal curve, what is the z score below which 20% of the area falls?

IMPLICATIONS OF THE NORMAL CURVE

Here, we will discuss some important implications of the normal curve in the field of educational research.

To Determine Percentage of the Case Within Given Limits

Many times we need to find what proportion of cases falls within two given scores. If the distribution is normal. We can use table of area under normal curve to find such proportions. First we convert the given raw score limits into z-score limits by using transformation.

$$z = \frac{x - \mu}{\sigma}$$

Using table of area, one find the area between these z-score limits.

Example 3:

What proportion of scores falls between $x = 88$ and $x = 95$ if the normal distribution x has a mean of 85 and standard deviation of 5.

Solution:

The distribution of x is shown in Fig. 4.7.

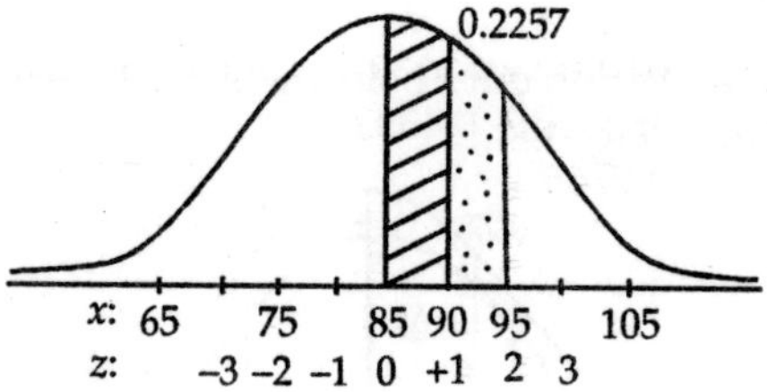

Fig. 4.7

First convert 88 and 95 to z-score.

$$z_1 = \frac{x_1 - \mu}{\sigma}$$

$$= \frac{88-85}{5} = 0.60$$

$$z_2 = \frac{x_2 - \mu}{\sigma}$$

$$= \frac{95-85}{5} = 2.00$$

we want to find

$$P(88 < x < 95) = P(0.60 < z < 2.0)$$
$$= P(0 < z < 2.0) - P(0 < z < .60)$$
$$= 0.4772 - 0.2257 \text{ (from table of area of normal curve)}$$
$$= 0.2515$$

Therefore, the proportion of score between 88 and 95 is 0.2515.

Exercises

1. 1000 students appeared in an examination. Distribution of score is assumed to be normal with mean $\mu = 30$ and $\sigma = 625$. How many students are expected to get score (*i*) between 20 and 40 (*ii*) less than 35.

To Find the Limits Which Include a Given Percentage of Cases

This problem is reverse to the problem discussed in this Chapter earlier. Here, the area between two ordinate is given and we have to find the x-score. This can be determined by finding z-score corresponding to the area given, using table of area under normal curve and then converting z-score into x-scores.

Example 4:

In a normal distribution with mean $\mu = 45$ and standard deviation $\sigma = 10$, find the score below which 23% of the cases will fall.

Solution:

Here, we required to find out x below which 23% or 0.23 proportion of cases will fall in Fig. 4.8.

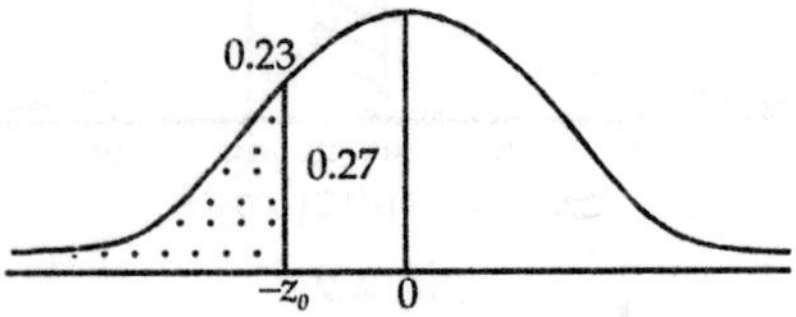

Fig. 4.8

We have to find the value of z_0 below which 0.23 area falls, i.e., the area between the ordinates at $z = -\infty$ and $z = z_0$ is 0.23. Hence, the area between the ordinates at $z = z_0$ and $z = 0$ is 0.27. Since the distribution is symmetrical, the same area 0.27 lies between the ordinates at $z = 0$ and $z = +z_0$. We see the table of area under curve, to find z_0 corresponding to which area is 0.27. This value is 0.74.

Therefore 0.23 proportion of area falls below $z = -0.74$. The x-score corresponding to $z = -0.74$ can be obtained by the transformation $x = \mu + \sigma z$.

$$
\begin{aligned}
x &= 45 + 10 \times (-0.74) \\
&= 45 - 7.4 \\
&= 37.6
\end{aligned}
$$

Therefore 23% of cases fall below $x = 37.6$.

Example 5:

If a distribution is normal with mean 100 and standard deviation 20, find out the two points between which the middle 60 per cent of cases lies.

Solution:

It may be seen from the Fig. 4.9— that the middle 60% of the cases are distributed in such a way that 30% of cases lies just below and 30% just above the mean.

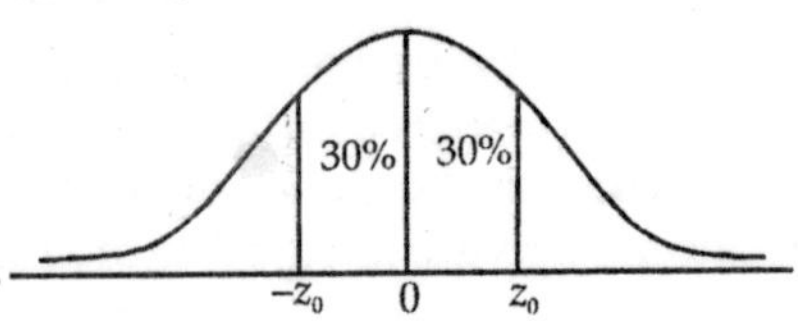

Fig. 4.9

From table of area under normal curve, we find that about 0.2995 cases out of 10,000 fall between the ordinates at $z = 0$ and

$z_0 = 0.84$. Similarly, 30% cases lies between the ordinates at $z = 0$ and $z_0 = -0.84$. Hence 60% of the cases lies between the standard scores of $z = -0.84$ and $z = 0.84$. We have to convert these standard score into raw scores.

Since, $$z = \frac{x - \mu}{\sigma}$$

Hence, the raw scores corresponding to $z = 0.84$.

$$0.81 = \frac{x_1 - 100}{20}$$

$$x_1 = 100 + 20 \times 0.84$$
$$= 100 + 16.8$$
$$= 116.8$$

Similarly corresponding to $z = -0.84$

$$-0.84 = \frac{x_2 - 100}{20}$$

$$x_2 = 100 - 20 \times 0.84 = 83.2$$

Therefore, middle 60% of the case lies between 83.2 and 116.8.

Exercises

1. In an examination the scores are found to be normally distributed with mean $\mu = 70$ and $\sigma = 8$. If 8 per cent of the students are in 1st division, what is the out off point for the first division?

To Determine the Relative Difficulty of Test Questions

In case of large group, the assumption about normal distribution of the ability of a group in terms of achievement on a test hold good. The percentage of cases who are able to solve a particular problem are counted from extreme right of the normal curve. If z_0 is the score corresponding to the proportion of the students solve the problem, z_0 may be treated as difficulty value of the problem.

Example 6:

Given a test problem solved by 10% of a large group, a second problem solved by 20% and a third problem solved by 30% of the same group. If we assume the capacity measured by the test problems to be distributed normally. What is the relative difficulty of questions 1, 2 and 3?

Solution:

For problem 1, divide the distribution into the parts such that 10% of the group lies above and 90% lies below the point. As shown in

Fig. 4.10 x_0 is the point such that 0.10 proportion lies extremely right and 0.50 proportion lies between the ordinates at mean and z_0.

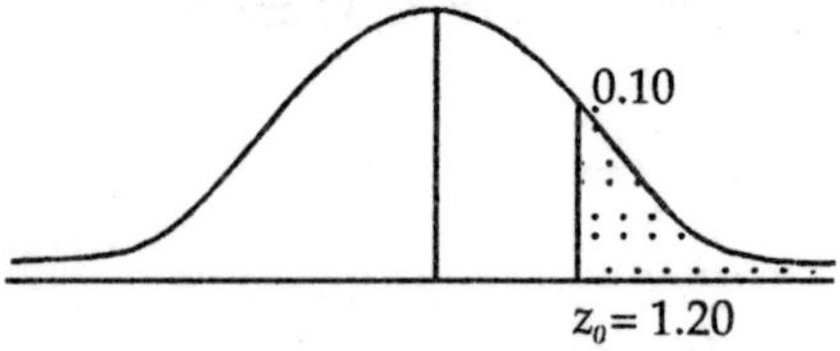

Fig. 4.10

Corresponding to area of 0.40, from the table of area under normal curve, $z_0 = 1.28$. Hence 1.28σ is the difficulty value of Question 1. For Question 2, 20% of the group, solved the problem. Hence 0.30 proportion, lies between the ordinate at $z = 0$ and $z = z_0$ and the corresponding z-score is 0.84. Hence 0.84σ is the difficulty value for Question 2. Similarly for Question 3, the difficulty values can be find out and it is 0.52σ. To summarise our results:

Question	*Passed by*	*σ-Value*	*Relative difficulty*
1.	10%	1.28	—
2.	20%	0.84	0.44
3.	30%	0.52	0.32

Hence, the relative difficulty between Questions 1 and 2 is 0.44 and between 2 and 3 is 0.32.

Exercises

1. Three problems 1, 2 and 3, passed by 50%, 60% and 70% respectively of large group. On the assumption of normality of distribution, find the difficulty value of test items 1, 2 and 3.

To Separate a Given Group into Subgroups According to Capacity

When certain trait is distributed normally, we can divide a group into subgroups according to capacity. Since the most of the area (99.73%) lies between –3σ and +3σ, we can consider that the base line of the standard normal curve extends from –3σ to +3σ. This total range of 6σ may be allotted to different groups according to given capacity and then the number of individuals can be found out according to the area bounded by the ordinates at these points.

Example 7:

Suppose that we have administered an entrance examination to 100 students. We wish to classify our groups into five subgroups

A, B, C, D and E according to ability, the range of ability to be equal in each group. On the assumption of normality, how many students should be placed in groups A, B, C, D and E.

Solution:

The base of the normal curve considered to extend from -3σ to 3σ. This range of 6σ may be divided into five equal parts. These five intervals may be laid of on the base line as shown in figure. Here A covers the upper 1.2σ, Group B the next 1.2σ, i.e., between $z = 0.6$ to $z = 1.8$, Group D lies between $z = -1.8$ to $z = -0.6$ and Group E lies lowest 1.2.

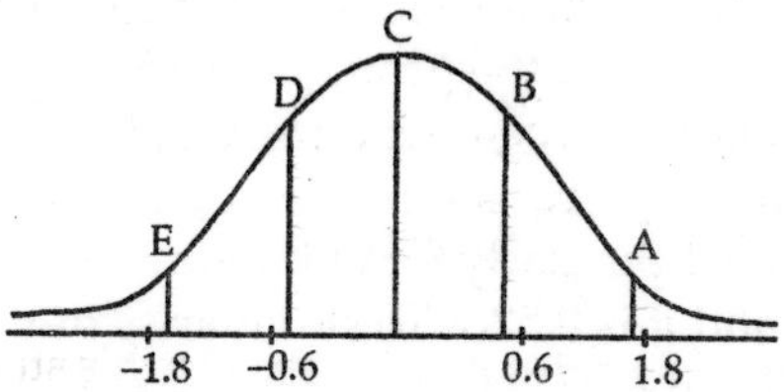

To find the percentage of whole group belongs in A, we must find the area bounded by the ordinates at $z = 1.8$ and $z = +3$, i.e.,

$$P(1.8 < z < 3.0) = P(0 < z < 3.0) - P(0 < z < 1.8)$$
$$= 0.4986 - 0.4641$$
$$= 0.0345$$
$$= 3.45\%$$

Similarly, the percentage of group belong in B, we find the area between the ordinate at $z = +0.6$ and $z = +1.8$

$$P(0.6 < z < 1.8) = P(0 < z < 1.8) - P(0 < z < 0.6)$$
$$= 0.4641 - 0.2257 = 0.2314$$
$$\text{or} = 23.84\%$$

Group C extends from $z = -0.6$ to $z = 0.6$.

The area of Group C is

$$P(-0.6 < z < 0.6) = P(-0.6 < z < 0) + P(0 < z < 0.6)$$
$$= P(0 < z < 0.6) + P(0 < z < 0.6)$$
$$= 0.2257 + 0.2257$$
$$= 0.4519$$
$$\text{or} = 45.19\%$$

Similarly the Group D and Group E extends from –0.6 to –1.8 and –1.8 to 3.0 respectively. Since the normal curve is symmetering, for Group D

$$P(-1.8 < z < -0.6) = P(0.6 < z < 1.8)$$
$$= 23.84\% \text{ (same as of Group B)}$$

and for Group E

$P(\angle 3 < z \angle -1.8) = P(1.8 < z \angle 3.0)$

$= 3.45\%$ (same as of Group A)

The percentage and number of students out of 100 in each group are given below:

Group	*Percentage (%)*	*No. of students (Out of 100)*
A	3.45	3 or 4
B	23.84	24
C	45.14	45
D	23.84	24
E	3.45	3 or 4

Exercises

1. A teacher assigned grades A, B, C and D to his students. If ability in Arithmetic is distributed normally, how many students of 500 should receive each grade?

Normal probability curve is the bell shaped, smooth symmetrical curve. Because the normal curve has so many useful mathematical properties, it is quite natural that we should exploit these properties in dealing with educational and psychological data. These properties have been discussed in the present Chapter. Normal curve has wide significance and applications in the field of Education and Psychology. The present chapter has dealt with these applications.

1. The correct answer is 'C'.
   (*i*) This should show an approximate normal distribution.
   (*ii*) The required area is shown in the Fig. 11.

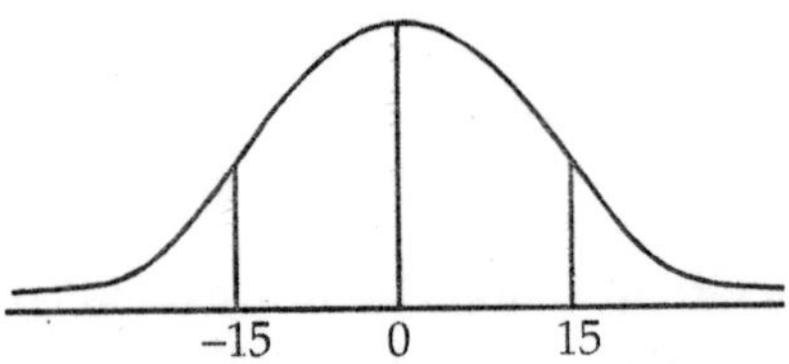

Fig. 4.11

we have to find.

$$P(-1.5 < z < 1.5) = P(-1.5 < z < 0) + P(0 < z < 1.5)$$
$$= P(0 < z < 1.5) + P(0 < z < 1.5)$$
(Since normal distribution is symmetrical).
$$= 0.4332 + 0.4332$$
$$= 0.8664$$

Hence, the area between z scores of –1.50 and +1.50 is 0.8664.

(*iii*) Here we require to find z_0 — the value of z score such that the area bounded by the ordinates at $z = -\infty$ and $z = z_0$ is 0.20 i.e.

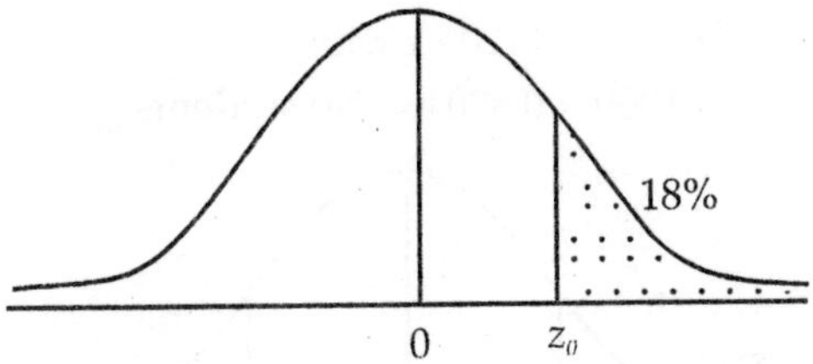

$$P(-\infty <_z <_{z0}) = 0.20$$
$$P(-\infty <_z < 0) = P(-z_0 < z < 0) = 0.20$$
$$P(z_0 <_z < 0) = 0.50 - 0.20$$
$$= 0.30$$

From table of area under normal curve, $z_0 = -0.84$

Hence, $z_0 = -0.84$ below which 20% of the area falls.

2.(*i*) In the first case, we have to calculate the proportion of cases lying between score x 20 and $x = 40$. The given distribution is normal with $\mu = 30$ and $\sigma = 6.25$. First we transform score 20, 40 into z score by the transformation.

$$z = \frac{z - \mu}{\sigma}$$

Let z_1 and z_2 be the standard score corresponding to $x = 20$ and $x = 40$ respectively.

$$z_1 = \frac{20 - 30}{6.25} = -1.60$$

and

$$z = \frac{40 - 30}{6.25} = +1.60$$

The distribution of x scores and standard scores is shown in Fig. 4.12.

The proportion of cases lies between score 20 and 40 is

$$
\begin{aligned}
P(20 < x < 40) &= P(-1.60 < z < 1.60) \\
&= P(-1.60 < z < 0) + P(0 < z < 1.60) \\
&= P(0 < z < 1.60) + P(0 < z < 1.60)
\end{aligned}
$$

(since normal curve is symmetrical)

$$
\begin{aligned}
&= 0.4452 + .4452 \\
&= 0.8904
\end{aligned}
$$

Therefore, the expected number of students scoring between 20 and 40

$$
\begin{aligned}
&= 1000 \times P(20 < z < 40) \\
&= 1000 \times 0.8904 = 890 \text{ students.}
\end{aligned}
$$

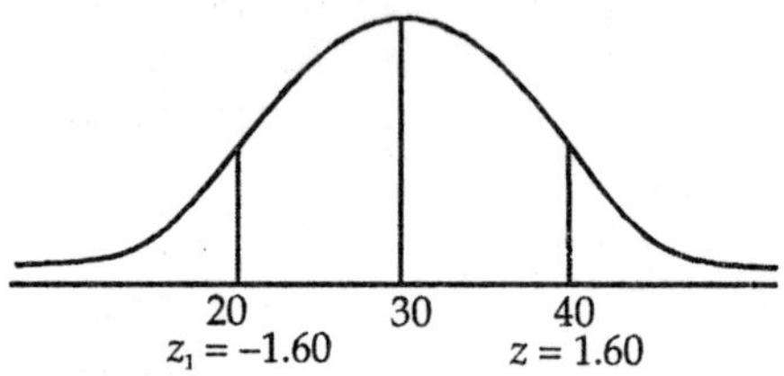

Fig. 4.12

(*ii*) In this case we require to calculate the number of students scoring below 35.

The z score corresponding to $x = 35$ is

$$z_3 = \frac{35 - 20}{6.25} = 0.80$$

We want to find

$$
\begin{aligned}
P(-\infty < x < 35) &= P-(-\infty < z < 0.80) \\
&= P(-\infty < z < 0) + P(0 < z < 0.80) \\
&= 0.50 + 0.2881
\end{aligned}
$$

(from the table of area under normal curve)

$$= 0.7881$$

Therefore, the expected number of students scoring below 35

$$
\begin{aligned}
&= 1000 \times P(\infty \times < 35) \\
&= 1000 \times 0.7881 \\
&= 788 \text{ students.}
\end{aligned}
$$

3. (*i*) An area of 18% or 0.18 corresponds to proportion of students receiving 1st division is on the extreme right of the distribution.

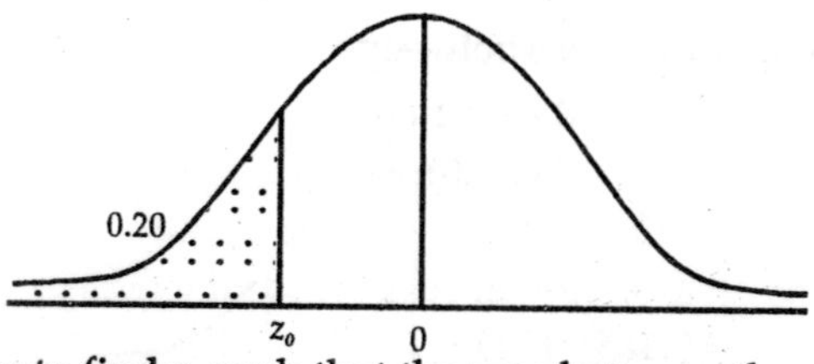

We have to find z_0 such that the area between the ordinates at $z = z_0$ and z = is 0.18 i.e.

$$P(z_0 < z < \infty) = 0.18$$
$$P(0 < z < \infty) = P(0 < z < z_0) = 0.18$$
$$P(0 < z < z_0) = 0.50 - 0.18$$
$$= 0.32$$

From the table of area under normal curve the value of z_0 corresponding to the area of 0.32 is 0.92, i.e., $z_0 = 0.92$ this $z_0 = 0.92$ is then converted to *x*–score by the transformation.

$$X = \mu + \sigma z$$
$$= 70 + 8 \times 0.92$$
$$= 77.36 = 78 \text{ (in whole numbers)}.$$

Thus a score of 78 is the lowest for securing 1st division in the said examination.

4. (*i*) In case of item 1, it has been solved by 50% of the group and of course 50% of the group has not been able to solve it. This item falls exactly in the middle of a normal distribution and z-scores is zero. Therefore the difficulty value of item 1 is zero.

In case of item 2, it has been solved by 60% of the groups. This item lies at a point in the distribution 10% below the mean. We find from the table of area under normal curve that 9.87% (roughly 10%) of the item lie between the z = 0 and z = –0.25. Therefore, the difficulty value of items 2 is –0.25σ. Similarly for last item 3, it has been passed by 70%, i.e., 20% more individual of group then the average. From the table of area, we find that 20% of this lie between z = 0 and z = –0.53. Hence, the difficulty value of item 3 is 0.53σ. The difficulty value of items 1, 2 and 3 are given below:

Item No.	*Passed by*	*z-score*	*Difficulty value*
1.	50%	0.00	00
2.	60%	0.25	–0.25σ
3.	70%	0.53	–0.53σ

5. (*i*) The position of four subgroups is represented on a normal curve.

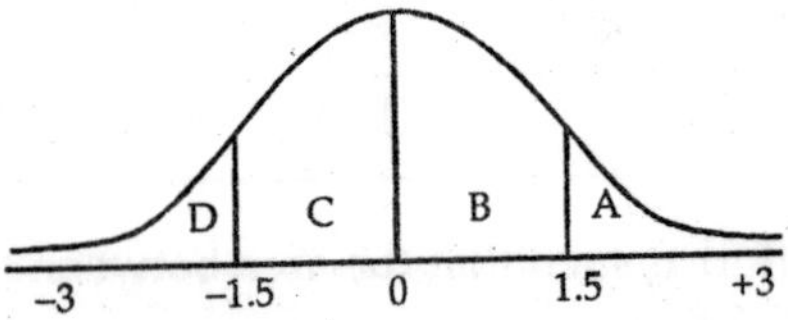

If the base line of curve is considered to extend from -3σ to $+ 3\sigma$, the whole range of 6σ may be divided equally into four. The Group A covers from 1.5σ to 3.0σ, the Group B covers from 0 to 1.5σ, the Group C covers -1.5σ to 0 and Group D covers from -3σ to -1.5σ.

To find the proportion of area covered by Group A, we require

$$P(1.5 < z < 3) = P(0 < z < 3) \ P(0 < z < 1.5)$$
$$= 0.4986 - 0.4332$$
$$= 0.0654$$

Numbers of students out of 500 belong to Group A

$$= 500 \times P(1.5 < z < 3)$$
$$= 500 \times 0.0654$$
$$= 32.70 \text{ or } 33 \text{ students.}$$

The proportion of area covered by Group B

$$P(0 > z < 1.5) = 0.4332$$

The number of students out of 500 belong to Group B.

$$= 500 \times P(0 > z < 1.5)$$
$$= 500 \times 0.4332$$
$$= 216.60 \text{ or } 217 \text{ students.}$$

Similarly the area under Group C is

$$P(-1.5 < z < 0) = P(0 < z < 1.5)$$
$$= 0.4332 \text{ (same as of Group B)}$$

And the number of students belong to Group C

$$= 500 \times 0.4332$$
$$= 216.60 \text{ or } 217$$

Similarly for Group D the number of students will be same as in Group A, i.e., 33 students. Hence, the number of students in four groups out of 500 are:

Group	*Number of students*
A	33
B	217
C	217
D	33

5

Standard Error of Means and Significance of Difference

A 'population' is a collection or aggregate of entities or individuals such as animals, machines, plants, etc. A population can be finite or infinite in number and existent by hypothetical in character. To study the population characteristics or behaviour, instead of enumerating the entire population, a few individuals from the population which comprises a sample are observed. This process is termed as sampling and here sample characteristics are utilised to approximately determine or estimate the population.

For example, on examining a particular stuff, we arrive at a decision of purchasing or rejecting the stuff. The error involved in such approximation is known as *'sampling error'* and is inherent and unavoidable in any sampling scheme. There are various sampling schemes, but the most commonly used is that of random sampling. This is the sampling scheme in which each individual of the population has got an equal chance of being selected in the sample.

The population characteristics such as mean, median, standard deviation, etc., are known as *'parameters'* of the population while the corresponding characteristics of the sample are called *'statistic'*. To illustrate, suppose a researcher at a University is interested in knowing what proportion of students at the University smoke. To investigate this question, he asks the 50 students of a class whether or not, they smoke and finds that 20 of them do. Thus, the percentage of students who smoke in his class is 40 per cent. On the basis of this information he constructs the following chart to represent his problem:

Group	*Characteristic of concern i.e. Percentage of who smoke*
Population — all students of the University	***Parameter*** — Percentage of students at the University who smoke
Sample — all students of a class	***Statistic*** — 40 per cent of the class smoke

STANDARD ERROR (SE)

From a population possibly a large number of samples can be drawn. For each sample, we can obtain a statistic. The set of values of statistic so obtained, one for each sample, constitute a distribution which is known as *'sampling distribution'* of the statistic. The standard deviation of sampling distribution of the statistic is termed as *'standard error'* of that statistic. To illustrate, suppose we have a population of size N = 4, consisting of the ages of children who are admitted in a school. Their ages are 6, 10, 12, 14 respectively. Let us draw samples of size $n = 2$, then all the possible samples will be (6, 10); (6, 12); (6, 14); (10, 12); (10, 14) and (12, 14). Let the statistic of interest be the average of children, this statistic for each sample is:

$$\frac{6+10}{2} = 8;\ \frac{6+12}{2} = 9; = 9;\ \frac{6+14}{2} = 10;$$

$$\frac{10+12}{2} = 11;\ \frac{10+14}{2} = 12 \text{ and } \frac{12+14}{2} = 13.$$

Here the values 8, 9, 10, 11, 12 and 13 determine the sampling distribution of the average age of students who are admitted in the school. We construct the following table to compute standard error of this statistic.

Average age from each sample X_1 (years)	$X_1 - \overline{X} = X_1 - 10.5$	$(X_1 - \overline{X})^2$
8	–2.5	6.25
9	–1.5	2.25
10	–.5	.25
11	+.5	.25
12	+1.5	2.25
13	+2.5	6.25
$\Sigma X_1 = 63$		$\Sigma(X_1 - \overline{X})^2 = 17.50$

The sampling distribution has mean

$$\bar{X} = \frac{\Sigma X_1}{n}$$

$$= \frac{63}{6} = 10.5 \text{ years}$$

and standard deviation

$$S = \sqrt{\frac{1}{n}\Sigma(X_1 - \bar{x})^2}$$

$$= \sqrt{\frac{17.50}{6}}$$

$$= \sqrt{2.91} = 1.7 \text{ years.}$$

This value of *s*, i.e. 1.7 gives the standard error of average age of children who are admitted to the school.

Sampling distributions are of great importance in theory and practice of statistics. It is because of the fact that the sampling distribution has the following important properties:

Important Properties of Sampling Distribution

The important properties of sampling distribution are:

- The arithmetic mean of the sampling distribution is the same as the mean of the population from which samples are taken.
- The sampling distribution of mean has a standard deviation (or standard error) equals to the population standard deviation divided by the square root of the sample size i.e./ $\sqrt{n}$.
- The sampling distribution of the mean is normally distributed.

These properties of sampling distribution of the mean are derived from a statistical law known as the *'central limit theorem'*.

Thus, to compute the standard error of a mean, we need two items of information: the standard deviation of population σ and the size of the sample, *n*. It is computed by the following formula:

$$\sigma\bar{x} = \sigma / \sqrt{n}$$

For example, suppose the mean height obtained from a sample of 100 boys of a university is 64 inches and the standard deviation of the height of all the boys in the university is 3 inches. Then the standard error of the mean height is given by

$$\sigma\bar{x} = \sqrt{n} = \frac{3}{\sqrt{100}}$$
$$= 0.3 \text{ inches.}$$

But since we do not ordinarily know, so we estimate it from sample drawn from the same population. Then formula for calculation of standard error of mean is given by

$$S\bar{x} = \frac{S}{\sqrt{n}},\ S = \sqrt{\frac{1}{n-1}\sum_{i=1}^{n}\left(X_i - \bar{X}\right)^2}$$

Example 1:

A random sample of 10 boys had the I.Q.'s : 70, 120, 110, 101, 88, 83, 95, 98, 107, 100. Find the standard error of mean I.Q. of the boys.

Solution:

Here σ is unknown, therefore we estimate σ from the data by the formula

$$S = \sqrt{\frac{1}{n-1}\Sigma\left(x_1 - \bar{x}\right)^2} \text{ where } \bar{x}\frac{\Sigma - X_1}{n} = \frac{972}{10} = 97.2$$

we prepare following table to compute S

$X_1 - X_1$	$X_1 - \bar{x} = X_1 - 97.2$	$\left(X_1 - \bar{x}\right)^2$
70	27.2	739.84
120	22.8	519.84
110	12.8	163.84
101	3.8	14.44
88	–9.2	84.64
83	–14.2	201.64
95	–2.2	4.84
98	0.8	0.64
107	9.8	96.04
100	2.8	7.84
$\Sigma X_1 = 972$		$\Sigma\left(X_1 - \bar{x}\right)^2 = 1833.60$

Thus $$S = \sqrt{\frac{1}{9}(1833.60)}$$
$$= \sqrt{203.73}$$

Thus standard error of mean I.Q. is

$$= \frac{S}{\sqrt{n}} = \frac{\sqrt[2]{203.73}}{\sqrt{10}}$$

$$= \sqrt[2]{\frac{203.73}{10}}$$

$$= \sqrt[2]{20.37} = 4.514.$$

Exercises

1. Given a population with mean 50 and standard deviation 12. From this population random samples of size 4 are drawn. Find the standard error of mean.
2. The height of 10 teachers of a school are found to be 70, 67, 62, 68, 61, 68, 70, 64, 66 inches. Find the standard error of average height of the teachers.

TESTING OF SIGNIFICANCE

A statistical hypothesis may be defined as a statement about one or more populations which we want to verify on the basis of information available from a sample, e.g., let us say that the hypothesis with which we are concerned have to do with a sex difference in verbal comprehension ability. Logically, there are three alternatives: (1) males have more ability than females, (2) females have more ability than males, or (3) there is no sex difference concerned with the ability.

In terms of symbols, these three alternatives may be expressed as follows: $\mu_1 > \mu_2$, $\mu_1 < \mu_2$ and $\mu_1 = \mu_2$, where the μs stand for population means and the subscript 1 denotes male and 2 female. A very important aspect of sampling theory is the study of tests of significance which enable us to decide whether the hypothesis is supported or not supported by the information available from the data. This is also known as *'hypothesis testing'*.

There are two statistical hypothesis involved in hypothesis testing. The first hypothesis to be tested usually referred as *'null hypothesis'* or 'hypothesis of no difference' and designed by H_0. In the above example, the first-two statements appear to be biased since they reflect a preferential attitude to ability of one or the other of two sexes. Hence the best course is to adopt the hypothesis of no difference as stated in (3) for testing. This is called null hypothesis and is given by $H_0 : \mu_1 = \mu_2$. Now, in the testing process this hypothesis is either rejected or not rejected. If the null hypothesis is not rejected, we will say that the data on which the test is based do not provide sufficient evidence to cause rejection. If the null hypothesis is rejected, we will conclude that the data at hand are not compatible with the null hypothesis, but are supportive of some other hypothesis. This other hypothesis is known as *'alternative hypothesis'* and designated by H_Δ or H_1. In the above example, alternative hypothesis could be $H_1 : \mu_1 > \mu_2$ or $H_1: \mu_1 < \mu_2$ or $H_1: \mu_1 \neq \mu_2$.

Then, a statistic usually referred as *'test statistic'* is computed from the data of sample. The magnitude of this statistic decides whether to reject or not to reject the null hypothesis. The following is the general formula to compute the test statistic.

$$\text{Test statistic} = \frac{\text{relevant statistic-hypotherized parameter}}{\text{standard error of relevant statistic}}$$

All the possible values that a statistic can assume are points on the horizontal axis of the graph of the distribution of the test statistic and are divided into two groups, one group constitutes what is known as the *'rejection region'* and the other group makes up the *'acceptance region'*. We reject the null hypothesis if the value of test statistic that we compute from our sample is one of the values in the rejection region and accept the null hypothesis if the computed value of the test statistic is one of the values in the acceptance region. It may be seen from the Fig. 5.0.

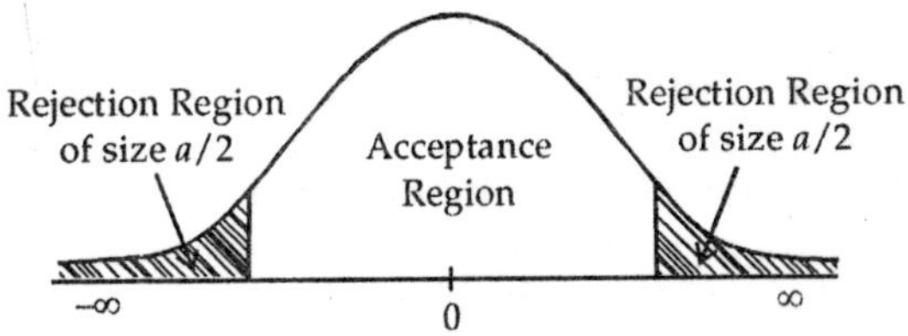

Fig. 5.0

The decision as to which values go into the rejection region and which ones go into acceptance region is made on the basis of desired *'level of significance'* designated by 'a'. The term 'level of significance' reflects the fact that hypothesis tests are sometimes called significance tests and a computed value of the tests statistic that falls in the rejection region is said to be significant. The level of significance, a, specifies the area under the curve of the distribution of the test statistic that constitutes the rejection region.

In the above figure, shaded area gives the rejection region whose total area is, i.e., $a/2$ on left hand side and $a/2$ on right hand side. It is seen, then that ∞ is the probability of rejecting a true null hypothesis. Since to reject a true null hypothesis would constitute an error, we should make probability of this error small and in fact that what is done. We usually take it .01, .05 or .10.

Testing of Significance of Difference of Means

Hypothesis testing or testing of significance involving difference between two population means is most frequently used to determine whether or not it is reasonable to conclude that the two are equal. In such cases, following hypothesis is tested

$$H_0 : \mu_1 - \mu_2 = 0 \text{ or } H_0 : \mu_1 = \mu_2$$

and alternative hypothesis is taken as

$$H_1 : \mu_1 - \mu_2 \neq 0 \text{ or } H_0 : \mu_1 \neq \mu_2$$

It is possible, however, to test the hypothesis that the difference is equal to, greater than or equal to, or less than or equal to some value other than 'zero'.

In testing of each hypothesis, we require standard error of difference of means of two population which can be obtained from sampling distribution of difference of simple means. By virtue of 'central limit theorem', the sampling distribution of the difference of sample means, $\bar{x}_1 - \bar{x}_2$ of independent samples of sizes, n_1 and n_2 drawn from populations with means μ_1 and μ_2 and standard deviation σ_1 and σ_2, respectively, is normally distributed with mean $\mu_1 - \mu_2$ and standard deviation

$$\sqrt{\frac{\sigma_1^2}{n_1} + \frac{\sigma_2^2}{n_2}}$$

e.g., if $\sigma_1 = 3, n_1 = 3, \sigma_2 = 2$ and $n_2 = 4$, then standard error of difference of mean is given by

$$\begin{aligned} \text{S.E. } (\bar{x}_1 - \bar{x}_2) &= \sqrt{\frac{\sigma_1^2}{n_1} + \frac{\sigma_2^2}{n_2}} \\ &= \sqrt{\frac{(3)^2}{3} + \frac{(2)^2}{4}} \\ &= \sqrt{\frac{9}{3} + \frac{4}{4}} \\ &= \sqrt{3+1} \\ &= \sqrt{4} = 2. \end{aligned}$$

Thus, standard error of difference of means is 2.

If σ_1 and σ_2 are unknown, we estimate these from samples drawn from respective populations and the formula for standard error of difference of means becomes

$$\text{S.E.}\left(\bar{X}_1 - \bar{X}_2\right)^2 = \sqrt{\frac{S_1^2}{n_1} + \frac{S_2^2}{n_2}}$$

where $$S_1 = \sqrt{\frac{1}{n_1}\Sigma(X_1 - \bar{x})^2}$$

and $$S_2 = \sqrt{\frac{1}{n_2}\Sigma(X_2 - \bar{x}_2)^2}$$

Thus various tests of significance of difference of two population means can be discussed in two broad classes:

- When population variance is known.
- When population variance is unknown.

When Population Variance is Known

Let $\bar{x}_1$ be the mean of sample of size n_1 from a population with mean μ_1 and standard deviation σ_1 and $\bar{x}_2$ be the mean of an independent sample of size n_2 from another population with mean μ_2 and standard deviation σ_2. Suppose hypothesis to be tested is $H_0 : \mu_1 - \mu_2 = 0$. Then standard error of difference of two sample mean is

$$\text{S.E.}\left(\bar{x}_1 - \bar{x}_2\right) = \sqrt{\frac{\sigma_1^2}{n_1} + \frac{\sigma_2^2}{n_2}}$$

Then the test statistics is given by

$$Z = \frac{(\bar{x}_1 - \bar{x}_2) - (\mu_1 - \mu_2)}{\text{S.E. } \bar{x}_1 - \bar{x}_2}$$

Under the null hypothesis $H_0 : \mu_1 - \mu_2 = 0$,

$$Z = \frac{(\bar{x}_1 - \bar{x}_2) - 0}{\sqrt{\frac{\sigma_1^2}{n_1} + \frac{\sigma_2^2}{n_2}}}$$

$$= \frac{\bar{x}_1 - \bar{x}_2}{\sqrt{\frac{\sigma_1^2}{n_1} + \frac{\sigma_2^2}{n_2}}}$$

Now if we compute [Z]> the value of [Z] at some specified level of significance *a*, then we reject our null hypothesis, otherwise we accept the null hypothesis.

Example 2:

(*i*) Intelligence test on two groups of boys and girls gave the following results:

Groups	*Mean*	*S.D.*	*n*
Girls	75	15	150
Boys	70	20	250

Is there a significant difference in the mean scores obtained by boys and girls.

Solution:

Here $\bar{x}_1 = 75, \bar{x}_2 = 70, \sigma_1 = 15, \sigma_2 = 20, n_1 = 150$ and $n_2 = 250$ and

The null hypothesis is that there is no difference in the mean scores obtained by boys and girls, i.e., $H_0 : \mu_1 - \mu_2 = 0$.

First of all, we calculate standard error of difference of mean scores as follows:

$$\text{S.E.}\left(\bar{x}_1 - \bar{x}_2\right) = \sqrt{\frac{\sigma_1^2}{n_1} + \frac{\sigma_2^2}{n_2}} = \sqrt{\frac{(15)^2}{150} + \frac{(20)^2}{250}}$$

$$= \sqrt{\frac{225}{150} + \frac{400}{250}}$$

$$= \sqrt{1.5 + 1.6}$$

$$= \sqrt{3.1} = 1.761$$

Then test statistics is

$$Z = \frac{x_1 - \bar{x}_2}{\text{S.E. } \bar{x}_1 - \bar{x}_2} = \frac{75.70}{1.761}$$

$$= \frac{5}{1.761} = 2.84.$$

Let *a*. 01 be specified level of significance. Then the value of [Z] at this level of significance from the table is 2.58.

As computed value of [Z] i.e. 2.84 is greater than 2.58, the value of [Z] at .01 level of significance, we reject our null hypothesis. Thus, there is significant difference between mean scores obtained by boys and girls.

(*ii*) If $\sigma_1^2 \neq \sigma_2^2, \sigma_1^2$ and σ^2 is known, then standard error of difference of means of two population is reduced to

$$\text{S.E.}\left(\bar{x}_1 - \bar{x}_2\right) = \sqrt{\frac{\sigma^2}{n_1} + \frac{\sigma^2}{n_2}} = \sigma\sqrt{\frac{1}{n_1} + \frac{1}{n_2}}$$

Then test statistic will be given by

$$Z = \frac{\bar{x}_1 - \bar{x}_2}{\sigma\sqrt{\frac{1}{n_1} + \frac{1}{n_2}}}$$

Example 3:

The means of two single large sample of 1000 and 2000 members are 67.5 inches and 68.0 inches respectively. Can the samples be regarded as drawn from the same population of standard deviation 2.5 inches?

Solution:

Here $n_1 = 1000, n_2 = 2000$

$$\bar{x}_1 = 67.5 \text{ inches } \bar{x}_2 = 68.0 \text{ inches}$$

and $\sigma_1^2 = \sigma_2^2 = \sigma^2 = 2.5$ inches.

We have to test the hypothesis that the two samples are drawn from the same population of S.D. 2.5 inches.

The standard error of difference of means is given by

$$\text{S.E. } (\bar{x}_1 - \bar{x}_2) = \sigma\sqrt{\frac{1}{n_1} + \frac{1}{n_2}} = 2.5\sqrt{\frac{1}{1000} + \frac{1}{2000}} = 2.5 \times .0387$$

Then the test statistics is

$$Z = \frac{\bar{x}_1 - \bar{x}_2}{S.E.(\bar{x}_1 - \bar{x}_2)} = \frac{67.5 - 68.0}{2.5 \times .0387}$$

$$= \frac{-0.5}{2.5 \times .0387} = -5.1$$

Since calculated $|Z|$ is $-5.1 > 1.96$, the value of $|Z|$ at 5 per cent level of significance, therefore, the value is highly significant and we conclude that the samples are certainly not drawn from the same population having standard deviation 2.5 inches.

Exercises

1. A random sample of the height of 6400 Indians has a mean of 170 cm. and standard deviation of 6.4 c.m., while a random sample of heights of 1600 Americans has a mean of 172 c.m. and a standard deviation of 5.3 c.m. Do the data indicate that the Americans are on the average taller than the Indians. (Test at 5 per cent level of significance).

When Population Variance is Unknown

(a) Large samples (usually n > 30)

(*i*) If $\sigma_1^2 = \sigma_2^2 = \sigma^2$ (say) and the variance is not known, then its estimate based on both the samples drawn from respective population, is used. The pooled estimate is given by

$$\sigma^2 = \frac{n_1 s_1^2 + n_2 s_2^2}{n_1 + s_2}$$

where

$$s_1 = \sqrt{\frac{1}{n_1}\sum(X_1 - \bar{x}_1)^2}$$

and

$$s_2 = \sqrt{\frac{1}{n_2}\sum(X_2 - \bar{x}_2)^2}$$

Then standard error of the difference of means is given by

$$\text{S.E.}\ (\bar{x}_1 - \bar{x}_2) = \hat{\sigma}\sqrt{\frac{1}{n_1} + \frac{1}{n_2}}$$

The test statistic is given by

$$Z = \frac{\bar{x}_1 - \bar{x}_2}{\hat{\sigma}\sqrt{\frac{1}{n_1} + \frac{1}{n_2}}}$$

(*ii*) If $\sigma_1^2 = \sigma_1^2$, σ_1^2 and σ_2^2 are unknown, then these values are estimated from the sample values.

The standard error of difference of means becomes

$$\text{S.E.}\,(\bar{x} - \bar{x}_2) = \sqrt{\frac{s_1^2}{n_1} + \frac{s_2^2}{n_2}}$$

and the test statistic is

$$Z = \frac{\bar{x}_1 - \bar{x}_2}{\sqrt{\frac{s_1^2}{n_1} + \frac{s_2^2}{n_2}}}$$

Example 4:

A research team wants to study the effect of the stress of modern life on people whether the urban areas should have a higher divorce rate than rural areas because of the greater stresses involved in urban living. The team selected a random sample of 50 urban area and a random sample of 60 rural area and obtained the divorce rate for each area. The mean divorce rate for each was calculated as 28 and 25 respectively and standard deviation 6 and 5 respectively. Is there any significant difference between divorce rate of urban and rural areas?

Solution:

Here = $n_1 = 50$, $n_2 = 60$, $\bar{x}_1 = 28$, $\bar{x}_2 = 25$, $s_1 = 6$ and $s_2 = 5$.

The null hypothesis to be tested is that there is no difference in the mean divorce rates for urban and rural areas. The standard error of difference of mean divorce rate is

$$\text{S.E.}\left(\bar{x}_1 - \bar{x}_2\right) = \sqrt{\frac{s_1^2}{n_1} + \frac{s_2^2}{n_2}} = \sqrt{\frac{36}{50} + \frac{25}{60}} = 1.07$$

Then the test statistic is

$$Z = \frac{\bar{x}_1 - \bar{x}_2}{S.E.\left(\bar{x}_1 - \bar{x}_2\right)} = \frac{28.25}{1.07}$$

$$= \frac{3}{1.07} = .028$$

Since calculated $|Z| = .028 < 1.96$, the value of $|Z|$ at 5 per cent level of significance, therefore we conclude that there is no significant difference between mean divorce rates of urban and rural areas.

(b) Small samples (n < 30)

(*i*) Suppose $\bar{x}_1$ and $\bar{x}_2$ be the means of two independent samples of n_1 and n_2 items which have been drawn from the two normal populations having the same standard deviation σ and means μ_1 and μ respectively. In this case, standard error of difference of means of two populations is given by:

$$\text{S.E.}(\bar{x}_1 - \bar{x}_2) = \sqrt{\frac{1}{n_1} + \frac{1}{n_2}}$$

where
$$s = \sqrt{\frac{n_1 s_1^2 + n_2 s_2^2}{n_1 + n_2 - 2}}$$

$$s_1 = \sqrt{\frac{1}{n_1}\Sigma(X_1 - \bar{x}_2)^2}$$

and

$$s_2 = \sqrt{\frac{1}{n_2}\Sigma(X_1 - \bar{x}_2)^2}$$

Then the test statistic is given by

$$t = \frac{\bar{X}_1 - \bar{X}_2}{\text{S.E.}(X_1 - \bar{X}_2)} = \frac{\bar{X}_1 - X_2}{s\sqrt{\frac{1}{n_1} + \frac{1}{n_2}}}$$

If computed $|t| > |t|$ at $n_1 + n_2 - 2$ degrees of freedom at specified level of significance, we reject our null hypothesis and accept otherwise.

Here, it is necessary that the parent populations from which samples are drawn should be normal. It has also been assumed that the variances of two populations are same.

The *t*–distribution is used when sample size is generally 30 or less and the population standard deviation is unknown. This distribution is commonly called as student's *t*–distribution. This distribution has been derived mathematically under the assumption of a normally distributed population.

Main Properties of the *t*-Distribution

The *t*-distribution has the following main properties:

- It has a mean of 0.
- It is symmetrical like standard normal distribution about the mean.
- The value of *t* varies from minus infinity (–∝) to plus infinity (+∝).
- Compared to the normal distribution, the *t*–distribution is less peaked in the centre and has higher tails.

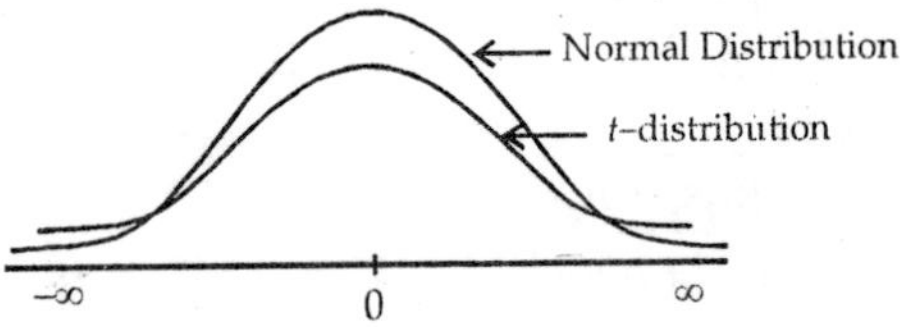

The number of independent variates which make up the statistic is known as the *'degrees of freedom'* (d.f.) and is usually denoted by μ (Nue). For example, if we are to choose any five numbers whose total is 100, we can exercise our independent choice for any four numbers only, the fifth number is fixed by virtue of the total being 100 as it must be equal to 100 minus the total of the four numbers selected. Suppose, if the four numbers selected be 20, 35, 15, 10, then fifth must be [100–(20+35+15+10)] = 20.

Thus, though we were to choose any five numbers, we have chosen only four. So our choice was reduced by one because of the one condition placed in the data, i.e., the total being 100. Thus, there are four independent variates and hence the degree of freedom were only four.

The degrees of freedom may also be considered as the number of independent observations, say n in the sample minus the number of parameters, say m required to compute the statistic which is estimated by sample observations. Thus $\mu\ n - m$, e.g., if $n = 10$ and $m = 2$, then degrees of freedom will be 8.

Example 5:

(*i*) For a random sample of 10 boys of a class fed on diet A, the increase in weight in pounds in a certain period were:

10, 6, 16, 17, 13, 12, 8, 14, 15, 9 pounds.

For another sample of 12 boys of a class fed on a diet B, the increase in weight in the same period were:

7, 13, 22, 15, 12, 14, 18, 8, 21, 23, 10, 17 pounds.

Test whether diets A and B differ significantly as regards the effect on increase in weight given that at 5 per cent level of significance, the value of it for 20 d.f. is 2.09.

Solution:

Here we have to test the hypothesis that there is no difference between the diets A and B as regards to increase in weight, i.e., $H_0: \mu_1 - \mu_2 = 0$. We prepare the following table to calculate standard error of difference of means:

X_1	$(X_1 - \bar{X}_2)$ $= X_1 - 12$	$(X_1 - \bar{X}_2)^2$	X_2	$(X_2 - \bar{X}_2)$ $= X_2 - 15$	$(X_2 - \bar{X}_2)^2$
10	–2	4	7	–8	64
6	–6	36	13	–2	4
16	4	16	22	7	49
17	5	25	15	0	0
13	1	1	12	–3	9
12	0	0	14	–1	1
8	–4	16	18	+3	9
14	2	4	8	–7	49
15	3	9	21	6	36
9	–3	9	23	8	64
			10	–5	25
			17	2	4
$\Sigma X_1 = 120$	$\Sigma(X_1 - \bar{X}_2)^2 = 120$		$\Sigma X_2 = 180$	$\Sigma(X_2 - \bar{X}_2)^2 = 314$	

From the table

$$\Sigma x_1 = 120, \quad \Sigma x_2 = 180, \quad \Sigma(x_1 - \bar{X}_1)^2 = 120, \quad \Sigma(x_2 - \bar{X}_2) = 314$$

$$\bar{X}_1 = \frac{120}{10} = 12 \text{ pounds}, \qquad \bar{X}_2 = \frac{180}{12} \text{ pounds}$$

$$s_1 = \sqrt{\frac{\sum(x_1 - \bar{X}_1)^2}{n_1}} = \sqrt{\frac{120}{10}} = \sqrt{12} \text{ pounds}$$

$$s_2 = \sqrt{\frac{\sum(x_2 - \bar{X}_2)^2}{n_2}} = \sqrt{\frac{314}{12}} = \sqrt{26.17} \text{ pounds}$$

Now
$$s = \sqrt{\frac{n_1 s_1^2 + n_2 s_2^2}{n_1 + n_2 - 2}} = \sqrt{\frac{20 \times 12 + 12 \times 26.17}{10 + 12 - 2}}$$

$$= \sqrt{\frac{120 + 314}{20}}$$

$$= \sqrt{\frac{434}{20}} = \sqrt{21.7}$$

$$= 4.66 \text{ pounds.}$$

Therefore, standard error of difference of means is given by

$$\text{S.E.}(\bar{x}_1 - \bar{X}_2) = s\sqrt{\frac{1}{n_1} + \frac{1}{n_2}}$$

$$= 4.66\sqrt{\frac{1}{10}+\frac{1}{12}} = 4.66\sqrt{\frac{6+5}{60}}$$

$$= 4.66\sqrt{\frac{11}{60}} \text{ pounds}$$

Thus, the test statistic is

$$t = \frac{\bar{X}_1 - \bar{X}_2}{\text{S.E. }(\bar{X}_1 - \bar{X}_2)}$$

$$= \frac{12-15}{4.66\sqrt{11/60}} = \frac{-3}{4.66} \times 2.34$$

$$= -1.51$$

Clearly, calculated value of $|t|$ is $1.51 < |t|$ at 5 per cent level of significance at 20 d.f. i.e. 2.09. So our null hypothesis is accepted and we conclude that there is no significant difference between diets A and B.

(*ii*) If $\sigma_1^2 \neq \sigma_2^2$ and they are unknown, then we estimate σ_1^2 and σ_2^2 from the samples drawn from respective populations. Then. standard error of difference of means becomes

$$\text{S.E.}(\bar{X}_1 - \bar{X}_2) = \sqrt{\frac{s_1^2}{n_1}+\frac{s_2^2}{n_2}}$$

$$s_1 = \sqrt{\frac{1}{n_1}\sum(x_1 - X_2)^2}$$

and $$s_2 = \sqrt{\frac{1}{n_2}\sum(x_2 - \bar{X}_2)^2}$$

In this case, test statistics is given by

$$t = \frac{\bar{X}_1 - \bar{X}_2}{\text{S.E.}(X_1 - \bar{X}_2)} = \frac{\bar{X}_1 - X_2}{\sqrt{\frac{s_1^2}{n_1}+\frac{s_2^2}{n_2}}}$$

Again here if $|t|$ calculated > $|t|$ at specified level of significance with $n_1 + n_2 - 2$ d.f., we reject our null hypothesis.

Exercises

1. In a test given to two groups of students, the marks obtained are as follows:

First Group:	18	20	36	50	49	36	34	49	41
Second Group:	29	28	26	35	30	49	46		

Examine the significance of difference between the arithmetic mean of the marks secured by the students of the above two groups.
(The value of t at 5 per cent level of significance for $V = 14$ is 2.14).

2. The scores of 8 urban and 7 rural boys in English are the following. Is the difference in the means of the two samples significant at .05 level.

Urban :	59	61	63	51	65	59	62	60
Rural :	60	62	60	64	59	58	64	

Testing of Significance of Difference of Pro ortions

If two samples are drawn from two populations, we may be interested in finding out whether the difference between the proportions of the some characteristics/attribute is significant or not. In such cases, we take the null hypothesis that whether the difference between P_1, the proportion of some characteristic/ attribute in one population and P_2, the proportion of the same characteristic/attribute in other population is 'zero'. Symbolically

$$H_0 : P_1 - P_2 = 0 \text{ or } H_0 : P_1 = P_2.$$

Then the standard error of the difference between sampl proportions P_1 and P_2 is obtained from sampling distribution of difference of sample proportion, and is given by

$$S.E.(P_1 - P_2) = \sqrt{\frac{P_1 Q_1}{n_1} + \frac{P_2 Q_2}{n_2}}$$

where $Q_1 = 1 - P_1$, $Q_2 = 1 - P_2$ and n_1, n_2 are the sample sizes.

If $P_1 = P_2 = P$ then this becomes

$$S.E.\ (P_1 - P_2)\uparrow = \sqrt{PQ\left(\frac{1}{n_1} + \frac{1}{n_2}\right)},\ Q = 1 - P.$$

Under the null hypothesis, the test statistic is given by

$$Z = \frac{P_1 - P_2}{\sqrt{PQ\left(\frac{1}{n_1} + \frac{1}{n_2}\right)}}$$

If calculated value of $|Z| >$ the value of $|Z|$ at some specified level of significance, we reject our null hypothesis, otherwise we accept null hypothesis.

In general, we do not have any information as to the proportion of same characteristic or attribute in the population, i.e., P is unknown, in that case, pooled estimate of population proportion P based on both the samples is used. The pooled estimate of P is given by

$$\hat{P} = \frac{n_1 P_1 + n_2 P_2}{n_1 + n_2}$$

Then standard error of difference of proportions becomes

$$S.E.(P_1 - P_2) = \sqrt{\hat{P}\hat{Q}\left(\frac{1}{n_1} + \frac{1}{n_2}\right)}, \hat{Q} = 1 - \hat{P}$$

Thus, test statistic will be

$$Z = \frac{P_1 - P_2}{\sqrt{\hat{P}\hat{Q}\left(\frac{1}{n_1} + \frac{1}{n_2}\right)}}$$

The conclusion can be drawn following the same argument as in previous sections.

Example 6:

Random samples of 600 men and 400 women were asked whether they like statistics, 325 men and 200 women responded 'yes'. Test the hypothesis that proportions of men and women who like statistics, are the same at 5 per cent level of significance.

Solution:

Here we have to test the hypothesis that difference of proportions of men and women who like statistics is zero i.e.

$$H_0 : P_1 - P_2 = 0.$$

Proportion of men who like statistics

$$= \frac{325}{600} = 0.54$$

Proportion of women who like statistics

$$= \frac{200}{400} = 0.50$$

Then the standard error of difference of proportion is given by

$$\text{S.E. }(P_1 - P_2) = \sqrt{\hat{P}\hat{Q}\left(\frac{1}{n_1}+\frac{1}{n_2}\right)}$$

where $$\hat{P} = \frac{n_1 P_1 + n_2 P_2}{n_1 + n_2} = \frac{600 \times 0.54 + 400 \times 0.50}{600 + 40}$$

$$= \frac{324 + 200}{1000}$$

$$= \frac{524}{1000} = 0.524$$

and

$$\hat{Q} = 1 - \hat{P} = 1 - 0.524 = 0.476$$

Standard error is

$$= \sqrt{.524 \times .476\left(\frac{1}{600}+\frac{1}{400}\right)}$$

$$= \sqrt{.524 \times .476 \times 10/2400}$$

$$= \sqrt{.001031}$$

$$= 0.323$$

Thus test statistic is

$$Z = \frac{P_1 - P_2}{\text{S.E. } P_1 - P_2} = \frac{.54 - .50}{.0323}$$

$$= 1.269.$$

Since (Z) = 1.269 < 1.96, the value of $|Z|$ at 5 per cent level of significance, we conclude that men and women do not differ significantly as far as liking of statistics is concerned.

Exercises

1. In a year there are 956 admissions in a school of which 52.5 per cent were boys while in school B, there are 450 admissions in the same year of which 43.4 per cent were boys. Is there any significant difference in the proportion of boys admission in school A and B?

The unknown characteristics of a population are approximated or estimated by the characteristics of sample drawn from the population. These approximations or estimations may involve some errors which are unavoidable. The sampling distribution of statistic is quite helpful in these approximations. Standard deviation of this distribution gives standard error of that statistic which plays significant role in testing of significance. Any testing of significance of hypothesis requires a test statistic which is decision-maker, i.e., whose value decides whether to reject or not to reject a hypothesis. This test statistic is defined as the ratio of the difference between statistic and hypothesised parameter with respect to standard error of that statistic.

Testing of significance of difference between means with the cases of known or unknown population standard deviation has been discussed in this chapter. Also, testing of significance of difference of proportions has been discussed. It has also been shown that the standard error plays a major role in these tests of significance. It is, in fact, the standard error which defines various tests of significance.

(*i*) $\sigma = 12.\ n = 4$

$$\frac{\sigma}{X} = \frac{\sigma}{\sqrt{n}} = \frac{12}{\sqrt{4}} = \frac{12}{2} = 6$$

(*ii*) Here $n = 10$ and $\bar{x} = \frac{\Sigma Xi}{n} = \frac{660}{10} = 66$ inches

x	$X - \bar{x}$	$(X - \bar{x})^2$
70	4	16
67	1	1
62	–4	16
68	2	4
61	–5	25
68	2	4
70	4	16
64	–2	4
64	–2	4
66	0	0
$\Sigma X = 660$		$\Sigma (X - \bar{x})^2 = 90$

$$S = \sqrt{\frac{1}{n-1}\sum(X-\bar{x})^2} = \sqrt{\frac{1}{9}(90)} = \sqrt{10}$$

$$\frac{S}{\bar{\bar{X}}} = \frac{S}{\sqrt{n}} = \sqrt{\frac{10}{10}} = 1 \text{ inch}$$

2. (*i*) $n_1 = 6400,\ n_2 = 1600$
   $\sigma_1 = 6.4, \sigma_2 = 6.3$

$$\text{S.E.}\left(\bar{X}_1 - \bar{X}_2\right) = \sqrt{\frac{(6.4)^2}{6400} + \frac{(6.3)^2}{1600}} = \sqrt{0.0064 + 0.0248} = 0.1767$$

and

$$Z = \frac{6.4 - 6.3}{0.1767} = 0.566$$

Since $|Z| < 1.96$ ($|Z|$ at 5 per cent level of significance). So we conclude that Americans are not on the average taller than the Indians.

3. (*i*) Here $n_1 = 9, n_2 = 7$

   Hypothesis to be tested is $H_0 : \mu_1 - \mu_2 = 0$.

   Here σ_1^2 and σ_2^2 are unknown and samples are small, therefore we will use the *t*-statistic.

x_1	$(x_1 - \bar{x}_1)$ $= x_1 - 37$	$(x_1 - \bar{x}_1)^2$	x_2	$(x_2 - \bar{x}_2)$ $= x_2 - 34$	$(x_2 - \bar{x}_2)^2$
18	–19	361	29	–5	25
25	–17	289	28	–6	36
36	–1	1	26	–8	64
50	13	169	35	+1	1
49	12	144	30	–4	16
36	–1	1	44	+10	100
34	–3	9	46	+12	144
49	12	144			
41	4	9			
$\Sigma x_1 = 333$		$\Sigma(x_1 - x_1)^2 = 1134$	$\Sigma x_2 = 234$		$\Sigma(x_2 - \bar{x}_2)^2 = 386$

Here $\bar{X} = \frac{\sum x_1}{n_1} = \frac{333}{9} = 37$ and $\bar{X}_2 = \frac{238}{7} = 34$

$$\text{S.E.}\left(\bar{X}_1 - \bar{X}_2\right) = s\sqrt{\frac{1}{n_1} + \frac{1}{n_2}}$$

where $$s = \sqrt{\frac{n_1 s_1^2 + n_2 s_2^2}{n_1 + n_2 - 2}}$$

$$s_1 = \sqrt{\frac{1}{n_1}\Sigma\left(x_1 - \bar{X}_1\right)^2}$$

$$= \sqrt{\frac{1}{9}(1134)} = \sqrt{126}$$

and

$$s_2 = \sqrt{\frac{1}{n_2}\Sigma\left(X_2 - \bar{X}_2\right)^2}$$

$$= \sqrt{\frac{1}{7}(386)} = \sqrt{55.1}$$

$$s = \sqrt{\frac{9 \times 126 + 7 \times 55.1}{9 + 7 - 2}}$$

$$= \sqrt{\frac{1134 + 386}{14}} = 10.42$$

Thus

$$\text{S.E.}\left(\bar{X}_1 - \bar{X}_2\right) = 10.42\sqrt{\frac{1}{9} + \frac{1}{7}} = 10.42\sqrt{\frac{16}{63}}$$

and

$$t = \frac{\bar{X}_1 - \bar{X}_2}{\text{S.E}\left(\bar{X}_1 - \bar{X}_2\right)} = \frac{37 - 34}{10.42} \times \sqrt{\frac{63}{16}} = \frac{3}{10.42} \times 1.984$$

$$= 0.571$$

$$\mu_0 = n_1 + n_2 - 2 = 9 + 7 - 2 = 14$$

Since calculated $|t|$ is less than 2.14. Therefore we conclude that the mean marks of the students of the two groups do not differ significantly.

(*ii*) Here $n_1 = 8, n_2 = 7$ $\Sigma x_1 = 480,$ $\Sigma x_2 = 427$

x_1	$x_1 - \overline{x}_1 = x - 60$	$(x_1 - \overline{x}_1)^2$	x_2	$x_2 - \overline{x}_2 = x_2 - 61$	$(x_2 - \overline{x}_2)^2$
59	–1	1	60	–1	1
61	1	1	62	1	1
63	3	9	60	–1	1
51	–9	81	64	3	9
65	5	25	59	–2	4
59	–1	1	58	–3	9
62	2	4	64	+3	9
60	0	0			
	$\Sigma(x_1 - \overline{x}_1)^2 = 122$		$\Sigma x = 427$	$\Sigma(x_2 - \overline{x}_2)^2 = 34$	

Here $$s = \sqrt{\frac{n_1 s_1^2 + n_2 s_2^2}{n_1 + n_2 - 2}}$$

$$s_1 = \sqrt{\frac{1}{8}(122)} = \sqrt{15.25}$$

$$s_2 = \sqrt{\frac{1}{7}(34)} = \sqrt{4.85}$$

$$s = \sqrt{\frac{8 \times 15.25 + 7 \times 4.85}{8 + 7 - 2}} = \sqrt{\frac{122 + 34}{13}}$$

$$= \sqrt{\frac{156}{13}} = \sqrt{12}$$

Thus

$$\text{S.E.}(\overline{X}_1 - \overline{X}_2) = \sqrt{12}\sqrt{\frac{1}{8} + \frac{1}{7}} = \sqrt{12} \times \sqrt{\frac{15}{56}}$$

The test statistic is

$$t = \frac{60 - 61}{\sqrt{12} \times \sqrt{15/56}} = \frac{-1}{\sqrt{180/56}}$$

$$= -\sqrt{\frac{56}{180}}$$

$$= -\sqrt{0.3111} = -0.56$$

Also

$$v_1 = n_1 + n_2 - 2 = 8 + 7 - 2 = 13.$$

The value of t at 13 df and 5% level is 2.16.

Since $|t| = 0.56 < 2.16$, so we accept our null hypothesis.

4. (*i*) Here $n_1 = 956, n_2 = 450$

$p_1 = 0.525, p_2 = 0.434$

Our null hypothesis is that there is no significant difference in admission of boys in the schools A and B, i.e., $H_0 : P_1 - P_2 = 0$. Here standard error of difference of sample proportions is

$$\text{S.E.}_{(P_1-P_2)} = \sqrt{\hat{P}\hat{Q}\left(\frac{1}{n_1}+\frac{1}{n_2}\right)}, \quad \hat{Q} = 1 - \hat{P}$$

where

$$\hat{P} = \frac{n_1 p_1 + n_2 p_2}{n_1 + n_2} = \frac{956 \times .525 + 450 \times .434}{956 + 450}$$

$$= \frac{956 \times .525 + 450 \times .434}{1406}$$

$$= 0.496$$

$$\text{S.E.}_{(P_1-P_2)\uparrow} = \sqrt{.496 \times .504\left(\frac{1}{956}+\frac{1}{450}\right)}$$

Thus, the test statistic

$$Z = \frac{P_1 - P_2}{\text{S.E.}_{(P_1-P_2)\uparrow}} = \frac{0.525 - 0.434}{0.027}$$

$$= 3.368$$

Since $|Z| > 3$, the null hypothesis is rejected and we conclude that there is significant difference in proportions of boys admission in two schools A and B.

6

Standard Score and T-Score

In this chapter, we shall consider some ways of transforming raw score scales into other scales for various reasons. One objective is to effect a more reasonable scale of measurement. Another important objective is to derive comparable scales for different tests. The raw scores from each test yield numbers that have no necessary comparability with the same numbers from another test. There are many occasions for wanting not only comparable values from different tests but also values that have some standard meaning. These are the problems of test norms and test.

Need of Common Scales

In psychology and education, it has been amply demonstrated that there are few, if any, absolute measures of human behaviour. The search for absolute measure has given way to an emphasis upon the concept of individual differences. The mean of the population has become the reference point, and out of the differences between individuals has come the basis for scale units. Even when the test happens to yield such objective scores as those in time, space or energy units, it is doubted that such units, although unquestionably equal in a physical sense, really represent equal psychological increments along scales of ability or performance. These considerations sends us in search of more rational and meaningful scales of measurement for behavioural events.

There is practical consideration that scales for different tests should be comparable. The most obvious need for comparable scales is seen in educational and vocational guidance, particularly when profiles of scores are used. The comparison of trait positions for a person depend upon having scores that are comparable numerically. For such a purpose, conversion of raw scores to values on some common scale is essential. Centile ranks make possible some comparable values for different tests. Centile values are ranks only, and do not represent equal units of individual differences. This limitation makes them less useful. It is possible to have scales that possess approximately equal units as well as comparable of means, dispersions, and form of distribution. The scales with comparability of means, dispersion and form of distribution are namely standard score scale, the T-scale and the stanine scale.

Standard Scores

If a student earns scores of 99 in Hindi examination, 25 in a reading test, 50 in a general academic aptitude test and 80 in general knowledge test. Is the student best in Hindi and poorest in reading? Could the student perhaps be equally good in all the tests? We cannot answer these questions on the basis of raw scores alone. If there are more than one student and we are interested in determining which student is more consistent in abilities and which one has the greater variability? Would a standard deviation of a student's raw scores give the answer? The reply to most of these questions is in the negative. We are extremely limited in making direct comparisons in terms of raw scores for the reason that raw scores are arbitrary and unique. We need a common scale before comparisons of the kind mentioned can be made. Standard scores furnish one such common scale.

CONVERSION OF RAW SCORES TO STANDARD SCORES

When mean and standard deviation of a test are known, we find the deviation of individual's raw score from the mean and divide these deviations by standard deviation (σ) of the test. Then these deviations from the mean expressed in (σ) terms are called (σ) score or (Z) scores or reduced scores. Thus a (σ) score or (Z) score is obtained from a raw score by means of the formula:

$$(Z) \text{ or } (\sigma) = \frac{X - \overline{x}}{(\sigma)} = \frac{X}{S}$$

Where,

X is raw score of the individual $\overline{x}$ is mean of the test scores
(σ) is the standard deviations of the test scores.

The mean of a set of (σ) scores is always zero and the (σ) is always unity. As approximately half of the scores in a distribution will lie below and half above the mean. Thus about half of obtained (σ) scores will be negative and half positive. In addition, (σ) scores are often small decimal fractions and hence somewhat awkward to deal within computation. For these reasons, (σ) scores are usually converted into a new distribution with a new mean and standard deviation so taken as to make all scores positive and relatively easy to handle. Such scores are called standard scores. This shift from raw to standard score requires a linear transformation. However, this transformation does not change the form of the distribution.

The formula for conversion of raw scores to standard scores is as given below:

$$\frac{X-M}{(\sigma')} = \frac{X-M}{(\sigma)}$$

$$X' = \frac{(\bar{\sigma})}{(\sigma)} (X-M) + M'$$

Where, X = a score in the original distribution.
X′ = a standard score in the new distribution.
M = Mean of the raw score distribution.
M′ = Mean of the standard score distribution.
(σ) = Standard Deviation of raw score distribution.
(σ') = Standard Deviation of the standard score distribution.

Following examples will show how the formula works.

Example 1:

Given a distribution with mean = 80 and (σ') = 20. Sohan's score is 90 and Geeta's 70. Express these raw scores as standard scores in a distribution with a mean of 300 and (σ) of 50.

The formula for standard score is $\bar{X} = \frac{(\sigma')}{(\sigma)}(X-M) + M'$

Substituting Sohan's score of 90 for X we have standard score X

$$X' = \frac{50}{20}(90-80)+300$$

Substituting Geeta's score of 70 for X, we have standard score X′.

Example 2:

Given a language test with a mean of 81 and (σ) of 12, and an arithmetic test with a mean of 33 and a (σ) of B. Mohan's score is 75 in language test and 29 in arithmetic. Assuming the distributions of language and arithmetic scores to be of the same form. Convert Mohan's scores into a standard score distribution with mean = 200 and (σ') = 20 and compare them.

Solution:

Sohan's standard score in language test

$$X' = \frac{20}{12}(75-81)+200$$

$$= 190$$

Sohan's standard score in arithmetic test

$$X' = \frac{20}{8}(29-33)+200$$

$$= 190$$

Thus Sohan's two standard scores are comparable and are equivalent.

Exercises

1. (*a*) Derive a linear conversion equation for transforming scores in the syllogism test into a scale that would give a mean of 50 and SD of 10.

Test:	Mean	SD	Student A	Student B
Syllogism:	28	8	30	15

   (*b*) Using the equation, determine the standard scores for students A and B on the new scale.

2. (*a*) The fifth-grade norms for a reading examination are mean = 60 and SD = 101 for an arithmetic examination are, Mean = 26 and SD = 4. Sonia scores 55 on the reading and 24 on arithmetic test. Compare her (σ) scores. In which test she is better?

   (*b*) Compare her standard scores in a distribution with mean of 100 and standard deviation of 20.

NORMALIZING THE FREQUENCY DISTRIBUTION: THE T-SCALE

When the distribution of scores is not a normal distribution then the obtained scores of a frequency distribution may be converted into a system of normalised (σ) scores by transforming them directly into equivalent points in a normal distribution. Equivalent scores indicates the same level of talent. The normalised standard scores are generally called T-scores. T-scaling was devised by *Mc Call (1939)* and first used by him in the construction of a series of reading tests designed for use in the elementary grades.

T-scores are normalised standard scores converted into a distribution with a mean of 50 and (σ) of 10. The T-scale begins at –5 (σ) and ends at +5 (σ) and T-scale ranges from 0 to 100; that its unit, i.e., T is 1 and that the mean is 50. T, of course, equals 0.1 of (σ) which is equal to 10. The reference point on the T-scale set at –5 (σ) in order to have the scale cover exactly 100 units. This is convenient but it puts the extremes of the scale far beyond the ability ranges of most groups. In actual practice, T-scores range from about 15 to 85, i.e., from –3.5 (σ) to 3.5 (σ).

DERIVATION OF T-SCALE EQUIVALENTS FOR RAW SCORES

The present distribution is of 520 scores obtained by B.Ed. testees in the achievement test in school organisation examination of the objectively scored type. The procedure for deriving T-scale equivalents for raw scores, as directed by *Guilford (1978)* was followed and Table 1 was prepared.

Table 1

The calculation of T-scores for a distribution of school organisation examination scores

1	2	3	4	5	6
Scores	*Upper limit of interval*	*Frequency*	*Cumulative frequency*	*Cumulative proportion*	*T-Score equivalent to*
35—37	37.5	1	520	1.00	—
32—34	34.5	7	519	0.998	78.7
29—31	31.5	50	512	0.984	71.5
26—28	28.5	66	462	0.904	63.0
23—25	25.5	68	396	0.732	56.2
20—22	22.5	102	328	0.636	53.5
17—19	19.5	75	226	0.432	48.3
14—16	16.5	61	151	0.282	44.3
11—13	13.5	52	90	0.160	40.1
8—10	10.5	25	38	0.076	35.6
5—7	7.5	11	13	0.026	30.6
2—4	4.5	2	2	0.004	23.5

The procedure for calculation of T-scores is explained step by step as given below:

Step I. List the class intervals in column 1. Here a large number of class intervals is desirable.

Step II. List the exact upper limit of class intervals in column 2.

Step III. List the frequencies in column 3.

Step IV. List the cumulative frequencies in column 4.

Step V. Find the cumulative proportions for the class intervals (column 4).

Step VI. Find the corresponding S-scores from Table 2 (This table is a standard table reproduced from Guilford (1978) page 480, Table No. (19.3) and write in column 6 of Table 1.

Table 2

An aid in the calculation of T-scores Reproduced from Gillford (1978) P-480

Proportion below the point	*T-score*	*Proportion below the point*	*T-score*	*Proportion below the point*	*T-score*
.0005	17.1	.100	37.2	.900	62.8
.0007	18.1	.120	38.3	.910	63.4
.0010	19.1	.140	39.2	.920	64.1
.0015	20.3	.160	40.1	.930	64.8
.0020	21.2	.180	40.8	.940	65.5
.0025	21.9	.200	41.6	.950	66.4
.0030	22.5	.220	42.3	.960	67.5
.0040	23.5	.250	43.3	.965	68.1
.0050	24.2	.300	44.8	.970	68.8
.0070	25.4	.350	46.1	.975	69.6
.010	26.7	.400	47.5	.980	70.5
.015	28.3	.450	48.7	.985	71.7
.020	29.5	.500	50.0	.990	73.3
.025	30.4	.550	51.3	.993	74.6
.035	31.9	.600	52.5	.995	75.8
.040	32.5	.650	53.9	.9960	76.5
.050	33.6	.700	55.2	.9970	77.5
.060	34.5	.750	56.7	.9975	78.1
.070	35.2	.780	57.7	.9980	78.7
.080	35.9	.800	58.4	.9985	79.7
.090	36.6	.820	59.2	.9990	80.9
		.840	59.9	.9993	81.9
		.860	60.8	.9995	82.9
		.880	61.7		

Step VII. Plot a point to represent each T-score in Table 1 (column 6) corresponding to the upper limit of the class interval (column 2) as in Fig. 6.1. If the original distribution of raw scores is normal, the points should fall rather close to a straight line. If they are not in straight line then draw through the points a line that will come as close to all the points as seems possible. Among those which do not touch the line, as many of them should be above it as below it. The line may be extended beyond the ends of the points at both ends. If the raw score distribution is skewed, the trend in the points will show some curvature (See Fig. 6.1).

It is then best to follow the curvature with a smooth trend. If the curvature is not followed, the distribution on the T-scaled score will not be normalised.

Step VIII. For any integral raw score point, find the corresponding T-score points from the graph (Fig. 6.1). These T-score equivalents of every raw score are given in Table 3.

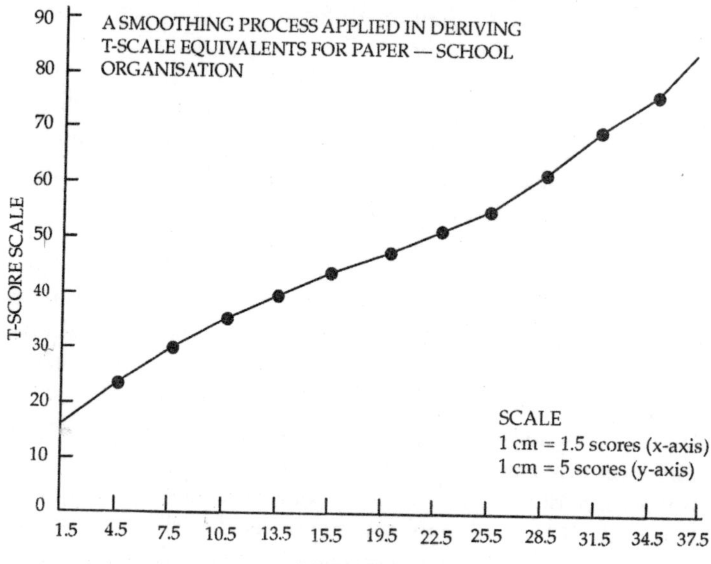

Fig 6.1

Table 3
T-score equivalents of raw scores for the distribution of school organisation paper scores (Read from graph, Fig. 6.1).

Raw scores	*T-scores*	*Raw scores*	*T-scores*	*Raw scores*	*T-scores*
2	18	15	42	28	62
3	20	16	43	29	65
4	22	17	45	30	67
5	24	18	46	31	70
6	27	19	47	32	72
7	29	20	48	33	75
8	31	21	50	34	77
9	33	22	51	35	79
10	35	23	53	36	83
11	36	24	54	37	85
12	37	25	56	38	88
13	39	26	58		
14	40	27	60		

Advantages of Standard Scores and T-Scores

The comparison of two students on different test scores can be made in terms of their standard scores. But in order to make accurate comparisons between different tests, two necessary conditions must be satisfied. Firstly, the population of students from which the distributions of scores arose must be assumed to have equal means and dispersions in all the abilities measured by the different tests. Secondly, the form of distribution, in terms of skewness and kurtosis must be very similar from one ability to another.

Thus in common scaling we have to proceed on the assumption that actual means, standard deviations and form of distribution are uniform for all abilities measured. In spite of these limitations, it is almost certain that derived scales provide more nearly comparable scales than do raw scores. Scores made by the same individual upon several tests cannot be compared directly owing to differences in test units. Thus a score of 120 on a group intelligence test and a score of 130 on an achievement test cannot be compared meaningfully. If scores like these are expressed as standard scores, however, they can be compared provided their distributions of raw scores are of the same form.

T-scores have general applicability and they cover a wide range of talent. T-scores from different tests are comparable and have the same meaning, since reference is always to a standard scale of 100 units based upon the normal probability curve. Moreover, T-scores are normalised standard scores converted into a distribution with a mean of 50 and (σ) of 10. When the scaling is carried out, the procedure normalises distributions and we achieve more common and meaningful scores. Other advantages of the T-scale have been possibility of extending it beyond limited populations, its convenient mean and standard deviation; and its general applicability.

Exercises

1. Calculate T-scores for the following raw scores.
   Raw scores : 10, 9, 8, 7, 6, 5, 4, 3
   Frequency : 1, 4, 6, 10, 8, 13, 18, 2
2. Can T-scale be extended beyond limited population?
3. Calculate T-scores for the following raw scores
   Raw scores : 91, 90, 89, 88, 87, 86, 85 84, 83, 82, 81
   Frequency : 2, 4, 6, 20, 24, 28, 40, 36, 24, 12, 4
4. Find T-score equivalents of raw scores for the following distributions:

Score	*Frequency*
17—18	4
15—16	45
13—14	90
11—12	87
9—10	127
7—8	94
5—6	50
3—4	16
1—2	7

There are various methods used in the scaling of psychological and educational mental tests data. Many of them are based upon the normal probability curve. As used in mental measurement, a scale is a continuum or continuity along which items, tasks, problems and the like have been located in terms of difficulty or some other attribute. The units of a scale are arbitrary and unique which depends upon the method employed by the researcher. Ideally, scale units should be equal, have the same meaning, and remain stable throughout the scale. Instead of scaling separate test items, it is usually saving of time and effort to scale aggregates of items or total scores. Here we have discussed two methods of scaling scores. These procedures are generally followed in constructing aptitude and achievement tests. They enable us to combine and compare scores originally expressed in different units. These are standard score and T-score methods.

In standard score conversion, the raw scores are first converted into (σ)—scores which are further converted into a new distribution with M and (σ) so selected as to make all scores positive and relatively easy to handle. This conversion from raw to standard score requires a linear transformation. This transformation does not change the form of the distribution, if the original distribution was skewed or normal, the standard score distribution will be skewed or normal in exactly the same fashion.

When we express scores made by the individual upon several tests as standard scores, they can be compared provided the distributions of raw scores are of the same form. T-scores are normalised standard scores converted into a distribution with a mean of 50 and (σ) of 10. T-scale ranges from 0 to 100. The reference point on the T-scale is set at –50 in order to have the scale cover exactly 100 units. This is convenient but it puts the extremes of the scale far beyond the ability ranges of most groups. In actual practice, T-scores range from about 15 to 85, i.e., from —3.5 (σ) to 3.5 (σ).

Exercises

1. (*i*) $X' = \frac{(\sigma')}{(\sigma)}(X - M) + M'$

   (*a*) Xs = 1.25 Xo +15
   (*b*) Xs = 52.5, 33.75

   (*ii*) (*a*) In neither, same score in both (*i.e.* –.5(σ))
   (*b*) Reading 90; arithmetic 90

2. (*i*) T-scores: 74, 67, 61, 56, 52, 48, 41, 29
   (*ii*) Yes.
   (*iii*) T-scores: 76, 71, 67, 62, 58, 54, 49, 44, 39, 34, 27
   (*iv*)

Raw scores	*T-scores*	*Raw scores*	*T-scores*
1	23	10	50
2	26	11	52
3	29	12	55
4	32	13	58
5	35	14	61
6	38	15	65
7	41	16	71
8	44	17	77
9	47	18	83

Bibliography

Anastasi, A.: *Psychological Testing*, New York, The Mcmillan Company, 1968.

Arkin, H. & Coltan, R.: *Tables for Statistician*, New York, Varnis & Novel Inc., 1950.

Cohen, Jacob: *Statistical Power Analysis for the Behaviour Sciences*, New York, Academic Press, 1977.

Downie, N.M. and R.W. Health: *Basic Statistical Methods*, New York, Harper and Row Publishers, 1970.

Fallik and Brown: *Statistics for Behavioural Sciences*, The Dorsey Press, Illinois, 1983.

Ferguson, G.A.: *Statistical Analysis in Psychology and Education*, McGraw Hill Book Co., New York, 1980.

Fisher, R.A. and Yates, F.: *Statistical Tables for Biological, Agricultural and Medical Research*, Edinburgh, Oliver & Boyd, 1963.

Garrett, H.E.: *Statistics in Psychology and Education*, McGraw Hill, Tokyo, 1980.

Guilford, J.P.: *Fundamental Statistics in Psychology and Education*, McGraw Hill Book Co., New York, 1973.

Guttman, Louis: *A Basis for Scaling Qualitative Data*, American Sociological Review, 9, 1944.

Hoyt, C.: *Test Reliability Estimated by Analysis of Varians*, Psychometrica, 1941, 6, pp. 153-160.

Kurtz, A.K. and Mayo S.T.: *Statistical Methods in Education and Psychology*, Narosa Publishing House, New Delhi, 1980.

Macnemer, Q.: *'Psychological Statistics', John Willey and Sons*, New York, 1962.

Mangal, S.K.: *Statistics in Psychology and Education*, Tata McGraw Hill Publishing Company Ltd., New Delhi, 1987.

McCall, R.B.: *Fundamental Statistics for Psychology*, Harcourt Brace Jovanovich Inc.: New York, 1980.

McCall, William A.: *'Measurement'*, Macmillan, New York, 1939.

Stanedecor, G.W.: *Statistical Methods*, Ames, Eyova State College Press, 1956.

Tete M.W.: *Statistics in Education*, New York, Macmillan Company, 1955.

Walker, H.M. and J. Lev: *Elementary Statistical Methods*, New York: Holt, Rinehart and Winston, Inc., 1958.

Index